# Cambridge Elements

**Elements in Semantics**
edited by
Jonathan Ginzburg
*Université Paris-Cité*
Daniel Lassiter
*University of Edinburgh*

# NATURAL LANGUAGE ONTOLOGY AND SEMANTIC THEORY

Kristina Liefke
*Ruhr University Bochum*

Shaftesbury Road, Cambridge CB2 8EA, United Kingdom

One Liberty Plaza, 20th Floor, New York, NY 10006, USA

477 Williamstown Road, Port Melbourne, VIC 3207, Australia

314–321, 3rd Floor, Plot 3, Splendor Forum, Jasola District Centre,
New Delhi – 110025, India

103 Penang Road, #05–06/07, Visioncrest Commercial, Singapore 238467

Cambridge University Press is part of Cambridge University Press & Assessment, a department of the University of Cambridge.

We share the University's mission to contribute to society through the pursuit of education, learning and research at the highest international levels of excellence.

www.cambridge.org
Information on this title: www.cambridge.org/9781009539272

DOI: 10.1017/9781009307789

© Kristina Liefke 2024

This publication is in copyright. Subject to statutory exception and to the provisions of relevant collective licensing agreements, no reproduction of any part may take place without the written permission of Cambridge University Press & Assessment.

When citing this work, please include a reference to the DOI 10.1017/9781009307789

First published 2024

A catalogue record for this publication is available from the British Library.

ISBN 978-1-009-53927-2 Hardback
ISBN 978-1-009-30780-2 Paperback
ISSN 2754-0367 (online)
ISSN 2754-0359 (print)

Cambridge University Press & Assessment has no responsibility for the persistence or accuracy of URLs for external or third-party internet websites referred to in this publication and does not guarantee that any content on such websites is, or will remain, accurate or appropriate.

# Natural Language Ontology and Semantic Theory

Elements in Semantics

DOI: 10.1017/9781009307789
First published online: December 2024

Kristina Liefke
*Ruhr University Bochum*

**Author for correspondence:** Kristina Liefke,
Kristina.Liefke@ruhr-uni-bochum.de

**Abstract:** This Element gives an introduction to the emerging discipline of natural language ontology. Natural language ontology is an area at the interface of semantics, metaphysics, and philosophy of language that is concerned with which kinds of objects are assumed by our best semantic theories. The Element reviews different strategies for identifying a language's ontological commitments. It observes that, while languages share a large number of their ontological commitments (such as to individuals, properties, events, and kinds), they differ in other commitments (for example, to degrees). The Element closes by relating different language- and theory-specific ontologies, and by pointing out the merits and challenges of identifying inter-category relations within a single ontology.

**Keywords:** ontology, compositional semantics, categories, semantic selection, intertheoretic relations

© Kristina Liefke 2024

ISBNs: 9781009539272 (HB), 9781009307802 (PB), 9781009307789 (OC)
ISSNs: 2754-0367 (online), 2754-0359 (print)

## Contents

| | | |
|---|---|---|
| 1 | Introduction | 1 |
| 2 | Identifying a Language's Semantic Commitments | 8 |
| 3 | Montague's Semantic Ontology | 33 |
| 4 | Larger Semantic Ontologies | 40 |
| 5 | Relating Different Ontologies | 52 |
| 6 | Conclusion: Finding the Perfect Ontology? | 58 |
| | References | 61 |

# Natural Language Ontology and Semantic Theory

> Do not forget that we are charting a jungle.
> (Vendler, 1967a, 705)

## 1 Introduction

To serve its core aims (i.e. explain acceptability, truth, and entailment), compositional semantics requires

(i) a domain of linguistic meanings, or *semantic values*;
(ii) the co-classification of similar (or similarly behaved) meanings, likely informed by grammatical distinctions; and
(iii) an account of the interaction of meanings from different classes.

Natural language ontology (or, more aptly, the ontology of natural language *semantics*) serves exactly this task: By providing a rich domain of nonlinguistic objects, it supplies the entities that serve as the semantic values of natural language expressions (see Lewis, 1972). By sorting these objects according to their truth-contributional, selection, and entailment behavior, it obtains semantic categories whose members interact with members of other categories in much the same way. In all this, natural language ontology is more than a mere bookkeeping system: it is what drives semantic theorizing. This is so since natural language ontology is influenced by our everyday metaphysics and results from applying engineering considerations (e.g. which ontological categories are used in day-to-day semantics?) alongside criteria of scientific theory choice. These criteria include which candidate theory is the most empirically adequate, predictively powerful, fruitful (such that it allows for easy integration with other accounts/theories), parsimonious (such that it contains as few basic categories as required), or simple (such that each category's elements have no or little internal structure).

Imagine being tasked to give a semantics for the simple English sentence in (1a). Clearly, this task involves (i) stipulating some semantic value for the lexical items *Matti* and *sleep* (possibly in the style of word-prime semantics[1]) and (iii) explaining how these values interact to generate the entailment to (1b) and the truth-conditions in (1c) (see Davidson, 1967):

(1)    a.  Matti is sleeping.
  ⇒  b.  Someone is sleeping.
        c.  *Matti is sleeping* is true  iff  Matti has the property of sleeping

---

[1] This term is due to Crouch and King (2008). Word-prime semantics parodizes an approach to semantics that specifies neither the lexical content of words or larger constituent expressions nor (at least initially) the particular ontological category to which this content belongs. The name 'word-prime semantics' derives from Carlson's report about Barbara Partee and Terence Parsons' 1976 UCLA course on Montague semantics, in which Partee carefreely identified the meaning of *life* as *life'* [read: 'life prime'] (see Carlson, 1977, foreword).

Importantly, in order to account for (1b) and (1c), we first need to (ii) determine to what ontological category the semantic values, ⟦Matti⟧ and ⟦sleep⟧, of *Matti* and of *sleep* belong. The identification of these values as members of one or other category influences the way in which these values interact to generate the compositional semantic value of the larger expression (thus affecting (iii)): depending on whether we categorize ⟦Matti⟧ as an individual (along the lines of Hendriks, 1993), as a generalized quantifier (i.e. a property of properties; along the lines of Montague, 1973), or as a property of individuals (along the lines of Fara, 2015; based on Quine, 1948), we obtain the semantic value of (1a) by attributing the property of sleeping to Matti (via backward Functional Application [FA]; see (2a)), by attributing the higher-order property of being one of Matti's properties to sleeping (via forward Functional Application; see (2b)), or by intersecting the property of being Matti with the property of sleeping (via Predicate Modification [PM]; see (2c)).

(2) a. ⟦Matti is sleeping⟧ = ⟦sleep⟧ (⟦Matti⟧)   (backward FA)
    b. ⟦Matti is sleeping⟧ = ⟦Matti⟧ (⟦sleep⟧)   (forward FA)
    c. ⟦Matti is sleeping⟧ = ⟦Matti⟧ ∩ ⟦sleep⟧   (PM)

It is widely acknowledged that the above categorizations of the semantic values of proper names (here, *Matti*) compete with respect to their empirical adequacy: While only ⟦Matti⟧'s treatment as an *individual* can explain why referential DPs – but not quantifier phrases – serve as the antecedents of anaphora (see (3)),[2] only its treatment as a *generalized quantifier* can easily explain the possibility of coordinating names (and other referential DPs) with quantifier phrases (see (4); based on Partee & Rooth, 1983). Finally, only by categorizing ⟦Matti⟧ as a *property* can we straightforwardly explain why proper names can have determiner heads (see (5)).[3] In (3b), the prefixed superscript '#' indicates that the ensuing sentence is semantically deviant.

(3) a. Matti$_i$ is sleeping. He$_i$ is snoring.
    b. {Every boy, No boy, More than one boy} is sleeping. #He is snoring.

(4) Matti and all other children are sleeping.

---

[2] Note, however, that anaphoric binding is a much more complex phenomenon than is suggested here for (3a) (see Fernando, 1993, and subsequent literature).

[3] The empirical trade-off between the different classifications of the semantic values of referential DPs is the key motivation behind the adoption of type-shifting principles (see e.g. Jacobson, 1999; Partee, 1987; Winter, 2002) and categorially flexible semantic theories (Charlow, 2014; Hendriks, 1993; see Section 2.1.2).

(5) a. Der Matti schläft. (German)
 The Matti sleeps.
 'Matti is sleeping.'
 b. There are two Mattis in my family.

Interestingly, the different categorizations of ⟦Matti⟧ also differ along other dimensions of scientific theory choice (what is sometimes attributed to the level of metasemantics; see Rett, 2022). In particular, ⟦Matti⟧'s categorization as an individual is simpler and more natural/intuitive than its 'generalized quantifier'- or 'property'-categorizations. Since it can be used to represent individuals as well as properties (see Partee, 1987), the categorization of ⟦Matti⟧ as a generalized quantifier is more uniform than its categorization as an individual or a property.[4] Given that we need properties and generalized quantifiers anyway (see (4), (5)) – and assuming that there is some way of explaining the deviance of (3b) without recourse to individuals – the 'property'- and 'generalized quantifier'-categorizations of ⟦Matti⟧ are ontologically more parsimonious than its categorization as an individual. The preference for a parsimonious ontology (with fewer categories) contrasts with the engineer's perspective on natural language ontology, which prefers as many categories as are assumed in day-to-day semantic practice.

This Element discusses which ontological categories are assumed in semantic theorizing, and identifies some of the parameters that influence the choice of categories. To avoid mixing empirical and foundational considerations, the Element identifies ontological categories from the perspective of semantic adequacy only. The result will be a practitioner's view of natural language ontology that captures what I call *descriptive* natural language ontology (in line with Strawson's (1959) *descriptive metaphysics*).[5] For type-theoretic attempts to reduce the categories in this ontology to a small subset, the reader is referred to the sequel Element, *Reduction and Unification in Natural Language Ontology*.

The Element is organized as follows: Section 2 reviews different strategies for identifying a language's semantic commitments.[6] The next two sections apply these strategies to (distinct fragments of) different natural languages – especially to Montague's PTQ-fragment (Section 3) and to its various extensions (Section 4). My application of these strategies will show that differently

---

[4] An analogous claim has recently been defended for the domain of clausal embedding (e.g. in Ciardelli et al., 2017; Theiler et al., 2018; Uegaki & Sudo, 2019).

[5] My distinction between descriptive and type-theoretic natural language ontology is reminiscent of Asher's distinction between a first level of semantic analysis (which identifies the rich ontology of natural language semantics) and a second level of semantic analysis (which provides a careful and more systematic account of the elements in this ontology; see Asher, 1993, 2).

[6] The term 'semantic commitment' is due to Wellwood (2020).

rich fragments of the same language – like similar fragments of different languages – presuppose in part different descriptive semantic ontologies. Section 5 identifies inclusion relations between these ontologies and proposes a strategy for 'translating' semantic accounts of a given phenomenon (formulated in a specific semantic theory, with a particular ontology) into a different ontology. The Element closes by summarizing its key points (commitment identification, candidate ontologies, inter-ontology relations) and by detailing to what extent a researcher's objectives can influence the resulting ontology (Section 6).

Before I move to a discussion of descriptive natural language ontology, it is important to be clear about the domain of natural language ontology and about the familiar motivations for exploring this domain. Sections 1.1 and 1.2 serve this task.

## 1.1 Ontology as 'Natural Language Metaphysics'

Natural language ontology was first introduced by Emmon Bach (1986b), who called this discipline *natural language metaphysics*. Bach chose the term 'metaphysics' to reflect the discipline's concern with "what there is" (see Quine, 1948), or, more accurately, with "what ... people talk as if there is" (Bach, 1986b, 573). To capture its focus on the different classes of objects that are assumed by our semantic theories – as well as on the relations between objects from these different classes – Bach's discipline is nowadays often called 'natural language ontology' (see, e.g. Ginzburg, 2008; Grimm & McNally, 2022; Moltmann, 2020a, 2022b; Ramchand, 2022; Rett, 2022). The use of this term is in line with the use of 'ontology' in data and computer science (where it serves the classification, description, and relation of entities from a specific domain). It is also in line with the use of 'ontology' in the applied field of ontology engineering.

An advantage of the term 'ontology' is that it can be used to refer both to the discipline and to its topic of study, that is, the semantic ontology of natural language. (The latter, but not the former, consists of different ontological categories like 'individual,' 'property,' etc.) Since the noun *ontology* has a plural form (i.e. *ontologies*), it allows for the possibility (discussed in Section 4.5) that the subject matter of natural language ontology differs from language to language (or between different fragments of the same language). To avoid having the term 'natural language ontology' do double duty, I hereafter follow Moltmann (2022b) in using 'natural language ontology' for the discipline and 'semantic ontology of natural language' (shortened to 'semantic ontology' or, simply, to 'ontology') for the subject matter of this discipline.

Natural language ontology is sometimes described as reflecting the ontological commitments of speakers of the respective language. Importantly however, such commitments are typically not the (explicit or implicit) commitments of *speakers* but of semantic *models* of the language (see Asher, 1993; Bach, 1986b; Moltmann, 2022b). Bach captures this observation when he describes the guiding question of natural language metaphysics as "What kinds of things and relations among them does one need in order to exhibit the structure of meanings that natural languages seem to have?" (1986b, 573). Rett (2022) reinforces Bach's point by noting, "[w]hen I discuss the question of how many basic entities or types there are, I view the issue as regarding the semanticist's toolbox, rather than a given speaker's i-language" (281).

The above notwithstanding, arguments for (or against) certain ontological categories are often also based on their cognitive or psychological plausibility. Thus, many semanticists and philosophers have eschewed highly abstract entities like vectors (Zwarts, 1997; see Section 4.3.2) and – to a lesser extent – manners (Schäfer, 2008; see Section 4.2.1). Inversely, the large psychological/neuroscientific plausibility of the category 'individuals' has led many researchers to resist Keenan's proposal to drop individuals in favor of properties as a basic ontological category (see Section 4.4). This resistance is supported by neuroscientific findings about 'concept cells' or 'Jennifer Aniston cells' (see Gross, 2002). The latter are single neurons that only signal to pictures of a specific familiar individual (e.g. a celebrity or a friend/family member; see Quiroga et al., 2005). Within linguistics and psychology, the psychological plausibility of various other kinds of categories has been discussed, for example, by Rips and Hespos (2019) (for object individuation), by Keil (1979) (for natural kinds), and by Dowty (1991) (for proto-roles).

Natural language ontology pursues a distinctively different project from mainstream philosophical metaphysics (what Fine [2017] has called 'foundational metaphysics'). Specifically, in contrast to metaphysics, natural language ontology does not aim to unravel the fundamental building blocks of reality (or 'what there [really] is,' to use the familiar term from Quine, 1948; see, e.g. Asher, 1993; Bach, 1986b; Moltmann, 2022b; Montague, 1969; Sider, 2011; Wellwood, 2020). Attendantly, it does not provide the domain of a theory of (the real-world reference of) linguistic expressions. This explains why the semantic ontology of natural language is often carefree about including elusive entities like fictional and abstract objects (e.g. Sherlock Holmes, Pegasus, beauty; see Hintikka, 1959; Moltmann, 2004), uninstantiated properties (e.g. being a unicorn; Montague, 1970), and impossible events (e.g. me watching myself swim at the time of my swimming; Vendler, 1979). It also explains why this ontology is not very worried about underspecified identity-conditions of its objects (see Asher, 1993, 5–8).

## 1.2 Role and Interest of Natural Language Ontology

Its different goal from philosophical metaphysics notwithstanding, natural language ontology has traditionally played a large role in revealing 'what there [really] is.' This role is reflected in Davidson's (1977, 244) observation that "[o]ne way of pursuing metaphysics is . . . to study the general structure of our language." It is justified by Emmon Bach's elaboration:[7]

> One of our main resources for coming to understand the world is, after all, language, a sort of tool box for doing whatever it is we want to do. Do the fundamental distinctions that are reflected in the overt and covert categories of natural language correspond in any way to the structure of the world? How could they not? (Bach, 1986b, 593)

In many cases, metaphysics' recourse to natural language ontology is motivated by the difficulty of obtaining the fundamental building blocks of reality through a direct inspection of reality.[8] This indirect approach is supported by the (comparatively) easy availability of semantic theories for natural language, or by the even easier – if less reliable – accessibility of the semantic intuitions of natural language speakers. Examples of a language-based approach to metaphysics include Kripke (1981) and Lewis' (1986) argument for possible worlds, Hacker's (1982) argument for the separation of events from individual objects, and Fine's (2003) argument for the distinction between material objects and matter. These arguments are based on the need to give a semantics for modal claims, on the selectional restrictions of different existence predicates (see Moltmann, 2020a), and on the selectional restrictions of nonmodal/nontemporal predicates like *well-made* or *Romanesque* (see Moltmann, 2022b).

Expectedly, natural language ontology is still not able to settle every metaphysical debate. This is, in part, due to the fact that the same linguistic phenomenon (even in a single language) can receive equally adequate interpretations in different ontologies (see Ritchie, 2016, who defends this claim for competing semantics for plurals). Applied to my example (1a) [*Matti is sleeping*], the ontologies from (6a–d) all account for the entailment and truth-conditions in (1b–c). (This holds at least so long as one ignores other criteria of scientific theory choice, like parsimony, simplicity, and fruitfulness; see Section 5).

---

[7] For more recent expressions of this position, the reader is referred to Ritchie (2016).

[8] The described recourse is thus analogous to a language-based approach in the philosophy of mind, which identifies mental content by investigating the meaning/ truth-conditions of attitude reports. For a recent, particularly clear, application of this approach, the reader is referred to Blumberg (2019).

(6) a. {properties}
   b. {individuals, properties}
   c. {properties, generalized quantifiers}
   d. {individuals, properties, generalized quantifiers}

To keep our choice of ontology from influencing our metaphysics, Ritchie (2016) has proposed to adopt a Principle of Carrying Commitments (PCC). This principle assumes that, in determining a language's ontological commitments, semantics with equal empirical adequacy should be given an equal voice (see Ritchie, 2016, 20). In virtue of this assumption, it holds that a (language or) linguistic phenomenon only determinately carries a commitment to a certain ontological category if all (!) competitor semantics for this phenomenon carry this commitment. Since the different ontologies in (6) only agree with respect to properties, PCC's application to (1) only determines an ontological commitment to properties.

Importantly, the extension of (1) to larger fragments of English already changes the above picture: Since quantifier phrases like *all other children* in (4) resist an interpretation as a property (or as an individual), a fragment that contains quantifier phrases already carries a commitment to properties and generalized quantifiers. While anaphoric binding phenomena like in (3) provide empirical support for (6d) – and against (6c) –, the ontology of a semantic theory may be underdetermined by the available evidence (for examples, see Ritchie, 2016 and Liefke, 2018). This underdetermination may be due to the absence of data that decides between candidate theories/ontologies (metaphysical underdetermination) or to the inaccessibility of this data (epistemic underdetermination). Considerations like the aforementioned show that natural language ontology is not only relevant for the philosophy of language and metaphysics but also for philosophy of science and for scientific theory and model building more generally (see e.g. Morreau, 2014; Thagard, 1978), for which it provides a good example.

I have noted at the beginning of this introduction that natural language ontology is concerned with the identification, classification, and interaction of linguistic meanings. This description correctly suggests that the ontology of natural language semantics is itself a case for ontology engineering: The ontologies of natural language semantics allow for the same treatment as large informational ontologies. The result is a complex taxonomy of entities with clearly specified roles, properties, and relations.[9] Arguably, the absence of

---

[9] For an example, see the database and ontology for Chemical Entities of Biological Interest, ChEBI (Degtyarenko et al., 2008; available at www.ebi.ac.uk/chebi/).

a lexical focus in formal semantics often effects a neglect of within-class relations (i.e. of relations that capture domain-specific knowledge). As a result, semantic ontologies are typically different from knowledge representation networks.

This completes my overview of the disciplines to which natural language ontology is most relevant. To justify the ontology (or ontologies) that are assumed by our best semantic theories, I next present some strategies that can be used to identify a language's semantic commitments.

## 2 Identifying a Language's Semantic Commitments

It is often assumed that different semantic theories presuppose different ontologies. This holds, for example, for the semantics from Davidson (2001) and Chierchia and Turner (1988), which posit events and, respectively, nominalized propositions. The initial assumption of pluralism notwithstanding, the ontologies of contemporary semantic theories converge to a surprising extent, however. This is due to the fact that a 'good' semantic theory typically covers a wide range of phenomena (thus excluding certain forms of metaphysical underdetermination) and that different languages share a large number of phenomena (such that there are no large-scale language-specific differences; see Section 4.5). This part of the Element reviews some of the strategies that have been used to identify a language's semantic commitments (in Sections 2.2–2.4). It also observes some interesting differences in the outcomes of these strategies (in Section 2.5).

Before I present the different strategies, it is important (i) to exclude a prima facie sensible route to identifying semantic commitments that yields unintended results and (ii) to identify assumptions about the syntax/semantics relation that underlie many of the considerations in this Element. Section 2.1 serves these two tasks.

### 2.1 Background Considerations

#### 2.1.1 A Nonstarter: Metaphysically Loaded Vocabulary

An intuitively plausible route to a language's semantic commitments runs through overt category attributions (e.g. (7)) or class-existence statements (e.g. (8)). It additionally – or alternatively – runs through 'ontological' sortals (i.e. predicates like *proposition* and *event* in (9a); see Moltmann, 2022a; Vendler, 1967b, ch. 5). In what follows, I call the former route the 'overt class' strategy. The latter is called the 'sortal' strategy.

(7) a. It is a fact that John sang the song.   (Vendler, 1967b, 136)

b. The collapse of the Germans was an event/a gradual process.
(Vendler, 1967b, 138)

c. John's kicking of the cat was a [deliberate] action.
(Vendler, 1967b, 138)

(8) a. There are individual objects.

b. There are events/states.   (Moltmann, 2022a, ex. (19a))

(9) a. Bill believes the proposition that the Earth is round.

b. In the event of rain, the parade will be cancelled.

c. The fact that the insulation failed caused the fire.
(Vendler, 1967a, 709)

A first challenge for the 'overt class' strategy from (7)–(8) is that our ordinary-language use of nouns like *fact* and *event* may differ from that of the technical ontological terms 'fact' and 'event' (see Vendler, 1967a). This challenge is aggravated by the observation that these nouns may even be paraphrased away (see Montague, 1969, 148, who has claimed that (10a) is equivalent to (10b)).[10]

(10) a. The event of the sun's rising occurred at eight.

b. The sun rose at eight.

An at least equally problematic challenge to the 'overt class' strategy lies in the observation that ontological support from constructions like (7) and (8) is limited to a proper subset of those categories that are commonly assumed as part of the semantic ontology. In particular, while category-attribution sentences like (7) and class-existence statements like (8) are acceptable – if not very natural – for concrete entities like individual objects and events, they are deviant for the vast majority of abstract and higher-order objects (see (11) for some variously deviant examples). In what follows, I will use prefixed double superscript question marks (as in (11a)) to indicate that a sentence is semantically very odd or questionable. A single superscript question mark (as in (11b)) indicates that the sentence is semantically slightly or moderately odd.

(11) a. $^{??}$There are generalized quantifiers.

b. $^{?}$There are degrees/manners/times.

---

[10] Note, however, that Montague's paraphrase was famously proven inadequate by Davidson (2001) (see my Section 2.4.2).

The 'sortal' strategy from (9) avoids the above problem by being applicable to concrete and abstract objects alike. However, this strategy is challenged by the observation (due to Prior, 1963, 1971) that sentences with the syntactic form of (9a) are often not equivalent to their 'sortal-free' counterparts. Thus, while (12a) describes Sally as standing in the fearing relation to a propositional *content* (namely, that Fido barks), (12b) describes Sally as standing in the fearing relation to a propositional *object* (namely, the proposition – qua abstract object – that Fido barks; see Moltmann, 2003; 2013a). Since they relate Sally to different attitudinal objects, (12a) and (12b) have different truth-conditions: In contrast to the truth-conditions for (12a), many of the conditions under which (12b) is true are rather contrived.

(12) a. Sally fears that Fido barks. (Güngör, 2022, ex. (3))
≠ b. ?Sally fears the proposition that Fido barks.

Nonequivalences like the one in (12) can also be observed for sentences with non-sortal DPs (in (13) and (14)): with the DPs *ordinariness, a unicorn*) and with DPs of the form '*the property of* [DP ]' (or '*the generalized quantifier denoted by* [DP ]'; see D'Ambrosio, 2023; Moltmann, 2004; Zimmermann, 2006b). In particular, the result, (13b), of substituting the DP *ordinariness* in (13a) by the linguistic designator of its intuitive semantic value, i.e. *the property of being ordinary*, is semantically quite odd.

(13) a. Ordinariness is boring. (Moltmann, 2004, ex. (12))
≠ b. ??The property of being ordinary is boring.

(14) a. Sally seeks a unicorn. (D'Ambrosio, 2023, ex. (10))
≠ b. ??Sally seeks the generalized quantifier denoted by 'a unicorn'.

I will not dive into the possible sources of Prior's puzzle here.[11] For the present purposes, it suffices to point out that these nonequivalences reflect the difference between ordinary entities and semantic values (this point is forcefully made in Zimmermann, 2006b).

### 2.1.2 Syntactic and Semantic Categories

My previous discussion has suggested a close correspondence between grammatical and semantic/ontological categories. This suggestion is reflected – to a varying degree – in Vendler's (1967b) lexical–syntactic investigation of

---

[11] Roughly, these include (i) the relational analysis of attitude reports (as binary relations between an agent and the semantic attitude complement), (ii) the identification of the semantic contribution and compositional behavior of CP- and DP-taking occurrences of attitude verbs, and (iii) the identification of the semantic values of CPs with propositions (see, e.g. D'Ambrosio, 2023; Forbes, 2018; Güngör, 2022; King, 2002; Liefke, 2019; Moltmann, 2022b; Nebel, 2019).

semantic category distinctions (see Section 2.2), in Montague's (1970) assumption of a syntax–semantics homomorphism (see Janssen, 1983; Zimmermann, 2018), and in Klein and Sag's (1985) method of type-driven interpretation (see Heim & Kratzer, 1998, ch. 3). Specifically, Montague assumes that all elements of the same syntactic category are interpreted in the same semantic domain. This is achieved by combining a 'semantic uniformity' constraint on the interpretation of lexical items with a map between syntactic and semantic composition rules.[12]

If Montague's homomorphism were an isomorphism (such that each semantic domain would interpret the elements of *exactly one* syntactic category; see Figure 1a), the strategies that will be discussed in Sections 2.2–2.4 would provide an easy, reliable route to identifying a language's semantic commitments (there: the commitments of a reasonably representative fragment of contemporary American English). In fact, the bijective relation between syntactic and semantic categories would make it possible to conduct the project of providing

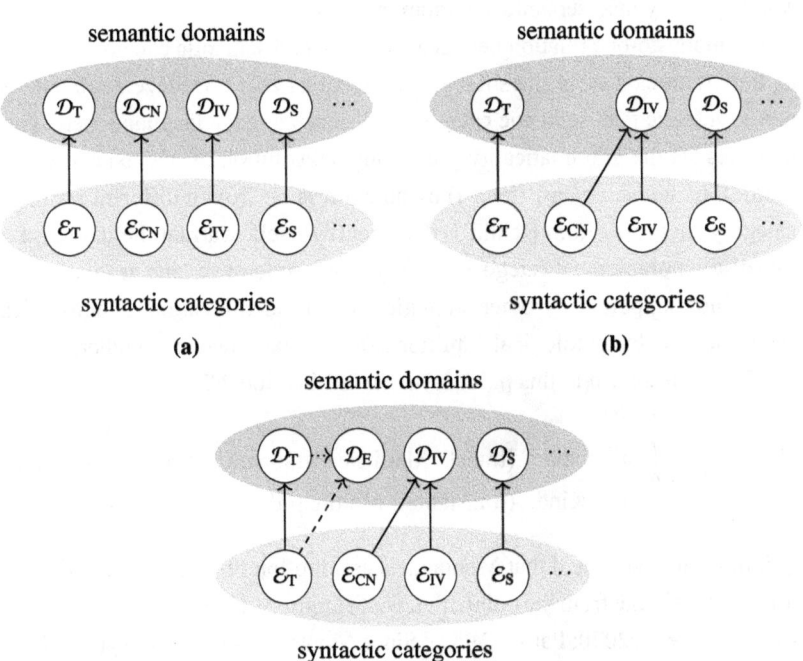

**Figure 1** The naïve (a), Montagovian (b), and flexible (c) view of the syntax–semantics relation.

---

[12] Montague's syntactic rules are rules of Categorial Grammar (Ajdukiewicz, 1935; Bar-Hillel, 1953; Lambek, 1958; see van Benthem, 1991).

an ontology for natural language at the level of syntax alone, without moving to semantic interpretation.

However, even Montague did not defend such a straightforward picture of the syntax–semantics relation. In particular, Montague's homomorphism is only surjective (i.e. 'onto,' as described in the penultimate paragraph), but not injective ('one-to-one,' in the sense described in the previous paragraph). As a result, a single semantic domain may provide the values of different syntactic categories. In Montague (1970), this is the case for intransitive verbs (IVs; e.g. *sleep*) and common nouns (CNs; e.g. *child*), which are both interpreted as properties of individuals. It is also the case for verb phrase adverbs (IAVs; e.g. *rapidly*) and infinitive-complement verbs (IV//IV; e.g. *try to*). An illustration of Montague's syntax–semantics relation is given in Figure 1b (adapted from Liefke & Hartmann, 2018, 319). In this figure, $\mathcal{E}_k$ is the set of expressions of syntactic category $k$ (where $k$ is a variable over categories); $\mathcal{D}_k$ is the associated set of semantic values. T is the syntactic category of DPs and quantifier phrases; S is the syntactic category of declarative sentences. Arrows represent Montague's syntax–semantics homomorphism.

The many-to-one relation between syntactic and semantic categories carries an important caveat for the strategies in Sections 2.2–2.3: Since there may be more syntactic than semantic categories, observing that a language (here: German) resists the grammaticality-preserving substitution of one expression (in (15a): German *schlafen* ['sleep']) by an expression from a different syntactic category (in (15b): *Kind* ['child']) does not, by itself, warrant the inference to two distinct ontological categories.[13] This holds at least so long as this distinction is not supported by other strategies for the identification of ontological categories, or by ontological intuitions (a fact exploited in Vendler, 1967a, 1967b). I will return to this point at the end of Section 2.2.

(15) Matti { a. schläft. (transl.: Matti sleep-3SG.SUBJ. 'Matti is sleeping.')
b. *Kind. (translation: Matti child  'Matti is a child.')

It has often been held that Montague's assumption of a surjective-only relation is undesirable from the point of view of simplicity (see, e.g. Charlow, 2014; Hendriks, 1993, 2020; Partee, 1987): Since Montague's theory of syntax, Categorial Grammar, identifies syntactic categories via the result of combining its expressions with an expression from a different category, all categories but S and the extensionally empty category *e* (intuitively, the category of

---

[13] This is supported by the fact that this argument would fail for languages (e.g. Tagalog, Samoan, and many sign languages) that do not have copulas.

individual-denoting terms) are complex (see Gamut, 1991, ch. 4.3; van Benthem, 1991). For example, since DPs (Montague's 'terms') combine with verb phrases (expressions of Montague's category IV) to yield a sentence (Montague's *t*; in Figure 1: category S), even referential DPs (e.g. *Matti, the boy*) are treated as members of a complex category.

As a result of the above, Montague's syntax–semantics map will require interpreting referential DPs in the same semantic domain as quantifier phrases, that is, as generalized quantifiers. Obviously, this strategy of 'generalizing to the worst case' (Partee, 1983, 34) goes against the principle of simplicity (reason: generalized quantifiers are internally complex entities).[14] What may even be worse: It violates basic intuitions about meaning and reference. According to these intuitions, proper names contribute their individual referents to the meaning of the linguistic constructions in which they occur (see Section 1.1 and Section 2.2.4).

To obtain the simplest-possible semantic ontology, this Element follows the inverse to the above strategy, namely, 'try simplest types first' (Partee, 1992, 115).[15] This strategy assumes that some subcategories (e.g. referential DPs) may allow for an interpretation as a simpler, less complex object (i.e. as an individual, associated with Montague's empty category E, originally *e*; see Hendriks, 1993, 2020). Such interpretations are obtained through a series of injective functions (called 'type-shifters') that map more complex entities to simpler entities while preserving their distinctness. An example of such a function is Partee's (1987) type-shifter LOWER, which sends a set of properties to the individual that exemplifies these properties. The syntax–semantics relation that results from this strategy is given in Figure 1c. In this figure, dotted arrows represent type-shifters. Dashed arrows represent the syntax–semantics relation that results from applying these type-shifters.

Arguably, not all linguistic expressions have their syntactic category written on their sleeve. This holds for example for the expression *a woman* in (16), which is ambiguous between the direct object of past-tense *see* and the subject of the gerundive small clause *a woman swimming* (for a more detailed discussion of this example, see Section 2.3).

(16)  Zeno saw a woman swimming.

---

[14] This strategy interprets an expression as an entity that is sufficiently complex/high type to accommodate (i) all uses of this expression (in different linguistic contexts) and (ii) all members of this expression's syntactic category.

[15] For an application of this strategy, the reader is referred to the introductory texts by Heim and Kratzer (1998) and by von Fintel and Heim (2021).

To prevent ambiguities like the one in (16) from distorting our investigation of semantic ontology, I identify 'syntax' with Logical Form, LF.[16] For the present purposes, I take LF to be the level of syntactic analysis at which ambiguities like the one in (16) are resolved and at which wh-movement and quantifier raising (if any) have taken place. An example of one of the LFs of (16) is given in (17). There, *a woman* has been raised out of the scope of the verb *see* (enforcing a *de re*-reading). In this raising, *a woman* has received a binder index (here: 1) and has left a trace ($t_1$) that has the same index as its binder. The square brackets around '$t_1$ swimming' indicate that this string is a syntactic constituent, identifying this reading with the small-clause reading.

(17)  [a woman]$_1$ [John saw [$t_1$ swimming]]

Arguably, working at the level of LF does not undo our observation that there is no royal road from syntax to semantics (and, hence, to ontology). This is so since a single constituent of an LF (e.g. *a woman* in some non-*de re* reading of (16)) may still be interpreted in different semantic domains (e.g. as an individual or a generalized quantifier).

In the following subsections, I will present several strategies for identifying a language's ontological commitments that try to avoid the most obvious syntactic fallacies. These strategies are based on the semantic selection properties of natural language predicates (see Section 2.2), on the study of dedicated pro-forms (see Section 2.3), and on the identification of implicit semantic arguments (see Section 2.4). They prevent counterintuitive conclusions (to too many, or too few, ontological categories) by focusing on <u>semantic</u> selection and semantic deviance (rather than on syntactic selection and syntactic inacceptability; in Section 2.2), by testing each strategy across a robust range of different constructions (especially in Section 2.3), and by moving away from language use (including language-specific selection and lexicalization) to language modelling (in Section 2.4). The separation of these strategies largely follows Asher (1993), whose classification of abstract entities considers "data about distributional differences and predicate incompatibilities" (see my Section 2.2) alongside "examples concerning anaphora" (Section 2.3) and quantification (Section 2.4; Asher, 1993, 4; cf. Rett, 2022).

## 2.2 The Lexical Strategy: Selection Properties

A first strategy for revealing a language's semantic commitments lies in investigating differences in the semantic selection properties of predicates. This

---

[16] Note that LF is a flexible notion that varies with the particular choice of syntactic theory.

## Natural Language Ontology and Semantic Theory

strategy assumes that selectional differences track ontological differences in the kinds of arguments that these predicates combine with. It associates different kinds of semantic arguments with different ontological categories. I will illustrate this strategy for the categories of facts and events (Section 2.2.1), questions (Section 2.2.2), propositions (Section 2.2.3), and individuals (Section 2.2.4), following the work of Vendler (1967a, 1967b).

Throughout this illustration, it is important to keep in mind that the selectional differences between predicates do not, by themselves, identify the specific ontological category whose elements these predicates accept as their semantic arguments. Rather, these differences show that different predicates only accept entities from an ontological category with certain properties. The identification of these entities as elements of one or another category is due to other considerations (e.g. everyday metaphysical assumptions about what kinds of objects exemplify these properties, the availability of certain category labels, and theory choice considerations; see Section 1.2).

### 2.2.1 Facts and Events

One of the best-known instances of the lexical strategy (due to Vendler, 1967a; Vendler, 1967b, ch. 5) has focused on selectional differences between different nominalizations. Such nominalizations include nominal gerunds like (18a), verbal gerunds like (18b), and *that*-clause constructions like (18c):

(18) a. i. the singing of the song ($ing_{of}$)

  ii. John's singing of the song (POSS-$ing_{of}$)

 b. John's singing the song (POSS-*ing*)

 c. that John was singing the song (*that*-clause)

According to Vendler, only nominal gerunds combine with perception and action verbs (e.g. *watch, listen to, imitate*), time-dependent existence predicates (e.g. *occur, take place, begin, last an hour*), and manner adjectives (e.g. *slow, sudden, gradual*) (see (19)). Only *that*-clause constructions combine with truth-evaluating predicates (e.g. *be true, be false*), propositional attitude verbs (e.g. *think, know, forget*), and speech act verbs (e.g. *state, claim*) (see (21); cf. Asher, 1993, ch. 1). In contrast to nominal gerunds, *that*-clause constructions also combine with modal adjectives (e.g. *possible, likely, good*) and causal predicates (e.g. *cause, make, be the result of*; see (20a, c)). In this respect, they resemble verbal POSS-*ing* constructions (see (20b)).

(19) a. The/John's singing of the song
b. ??John's singing the song  } occurred at noon/was sudden/loud/lasted an hour.
c. ??That John was singing the song

(20) a. ??The/??John's singing of the song
b. John's singing the song  } is unlikely/possible/made Mia blush.
c. That John was singing the song

(21) Mia thinks { a. ??the/??John's singing of the song
b. ??John's singing the song
c. that John was singing the song } or: is true/good.

The selectional difference between nominal and verbal gerunds is corroborated by the noun-like versus verb-like characteristics of these gerunds: unlike POSS-*ing* constructions (which require adverbial modification; see (22a)), *ing*<sub>of</sub> and POSS-*ing*<sub>of</sub> constructions only allow for adjectival modification (see (23a)).[17] In contrast to their verbal counterparts (see (22b–c)), *ing*<sub>of</sub> and POSS-*ing*<sub>of</sub> constructions are incompatible with auxiliary verb constructions (see (23b)) and with negation (see (23c); Grimm & McNally, 2022):

(22) a. John's singing the song *beautifully*
b. John's having sung the song
c. John not singing/having sung the song

(23) a. John's *beautiful* singing of the song
b. ??John's having sung of the song
c. ??John's not singing of the song

Vendler takes the different properties of nominal gerunds and POSS-*ing* constructions to suggest that these two kinds of gerunds are classified in different semantic categories. In particular, he assumes that nominal gerunds denote events, processes, and actions, while POSS-*ing* constructions denote facts or results (or, more generally, possibilities; see Ginzburg, 2005, fn. 11). Vendler motivates this categorization with respect to the specific properties of the predicates from (19) and (20): Since predicates like *occur*, *take place*, and *begin* express temporal properties, the semantic arguments of these predicates are temporal or temporally located objects, namely, events. Since predicates like *possible* and *likely* denote atemporal, modal, and causal properties, Vendler

---

[17] Recent work has provided several counterexamples to this generalization. These include the existence of nominal gerunds with adverbial modification (see, e.g. Alexeyenko, 2015).

identifies their semantic arguments with facts (esp. Vendler, 1967b, 141–146; see also Asher, 1993, for some cases).[18]

Note that the success of Vendler's argument for the event/fact-distinction relies on the selectional restrictiveness of the embedding predicate: while restrictive predicates like *occur* and *be possible* can be used to argue for a distinction between events and facts (as evidenced by (19)–(20)), selectionally flexible predicates like *surprise* (which license both nominal gerunds and POSS-*ing* constructions) challenge such an argument (see (24a–b); based on Vendler, 1967b, 125–126).[19]

(24)   a.   John's singing of the song   ⎫
       b.   John's singing the song      ⎬ surprised me.
       c.   That John was singing the song ⎭

I will show in Section 2.2.2 that the choice of embedding predicate plays an important role in Vendler's strategy for identifying semantic commitments: only selectionally restrictive predicates enable the identification of sufficiently fine-grained ontological categories. I will return to this point and discuss its extreme version in Section 2.2.4.

### 2.2.2 Questions

A parallel situation to the one in (24) can be observed for the ontological distinction between propositions and questions: Much work on the semantics of interrogatives distinguishes rogative predicates (i.e. predicates that only embed interrogative complements) like *wonder* (in (25b)) from anti-rogative predicates (i.e. predicates that only embed declarative complements) like *think* (in (25a); see e.g. Grimshaw, 1979; Lahiri, 2002). While the selectional difference between rogative and anti-rogative predicates supports the distinction between propositions and questions, the selectional flexibility of responsive (i.e. declarative- and interrogative-embedding) predicates like *know* (in (25c)) *prima facie* undermines it (see Ciardelli et al., 2017; Theiler et al., 2018):

---

[18] Vendler's semantic classification of POSS-*ing* constructions as facts is not uncontroversial. Alternative proposals for the semantic category of verbal gerunds include states of affairs (Zucchi, 1993), entity correlates of sets of minimal situations (Portner, 1992), possibilities (Asher, 1993, for other cases), fluents (i.e. primitive time-dependent properties; van Lambalgen & Hamm, 2005), and event types (Grimm & McNally, 2015). A philosophically inspired rejection of facts can be found in Betti (2015).

[19] Vendler's discussion uses deverbal genitive nominals (e.g. *John's death*) rather than -*ing*$_{of}$ constructions (e.g. *the passing of John*).

(25) Mia { a. thinks {i. that, ii.$^{??}$whether}
         b. wonders {i.$^{??}$that, ii. whether} } John was singing the
         c. knows {i. that, ii. whether}                            song.

For further empirical support for the distinction between propositions, facts, and questions, the reader is referred to Ginzburg (1995).

### 2.2.3 Propositions

Much of Vendler's work discusses the semantic difference between facts and events. Vendler (1967a) complements this discussion with two arguments for a distinction between facts and propositions. The first of these arguments targets a difference in the licensing predicates for POSS-*ing* and *that*-clause constructions. The second argument targets a difference in the intensionality properties of embeddings under POSS-*ing*- and *that*-clause-licensing predicates.

Vendler's first argument is based on the observation that only *that*-clause constructions felicitously combine with propositional attitude verbs (e.g. *think, know*) and with truth-evaluating predicates (see (21) and its surrounding discussion). Vendler's second argument is based on the observation that the choice of embedding predicate affects the referential transparency of the sentence containing this predicate (Vendler, 1967a, 709–712; see Asher, 1993, 58): While propositional attitude verbs famously create opaque contexts (i.e. contexts in which the substitution of co-referential or truth-conditionally equivalent expressions does not necessarily preserve the truth of the original sentence; see, for example, Forbes, 2006; Frege, 1997; Quine, 1956), this is not the case for causal predicates. Specifically, in contrast to (26), substituting *Jocasta* for *his* [= *Oedipus'*] *mother* in (27) preserves the truth of the original sentence (see also Davidson, 2001):[20]

(26) a. Oedipus knew that he was marrying Jocasta.
     b. Jocasta is Oedipus' mother.
     ⇏ c. Oedipus knew that he was marrying his mother.                  (invalid)

(27) a. The tragedy was caused by Oedipus' marrying his mother.
     b. Jocasta is Oedipus' mother.
     ⇒ c. The tragedy was caused by Oedipus' marrying Jocasta.           (valid)

---

[20] To avoid that the clause '*that Oedipus was marrying* [DP]' serves double duty as a proposition and a fact, I have replaced the *that*-clause in Vendler's (1967a, 709–710) example of a referentially transparent context (i.e. (27)) by a POSS-*ing* construction.

Newer literature supports the difference between propositions and facts by referring to the different cancellation behavior of non-factively embedded *that*-clauses and DPs of the form '*the fact that* [TP ]' (see e.g. Kastner, 2015). Thus, in contrast to the *that*-clause construction in (28a), the *fact*-DP in (28b) cannot be consistently negated. The non-negatability of *fact*-DPs straightforwardly extends to POSS-*ing* constructions (see (28c)), as Vendler's analysis would lead one to expect.

(28)  a. I explained that the building collapsed. (But it didn't really.)

  b. I explained *the fact* that the building collapsed. (#But it didn't really.)

  c. I explained the building's collapsing. (#But the building didn't really collapse.)

### 2.2.4 Individuals

Plausibly, Vendler's selection-based strategy can also be applied to distinguish individuals from events (see Vendler, 1967b, 143–144). In particular, in contrast to *ing*$_{of}$ and POSS-*ing*$_{of}$ constructions, concrete referential DPs can combine with adjectives for visually perceivable properties (e.g. color, size, shape, and texture; see (29a)), with object-directed perception verbs (e.g. *touch*, *look at*; see (30a)), and with extensional transitive verbs like *pull* and *kick* (see (31a)). To show that the referents of concrete referential DPs also resist a co-categorization with facts and propositions, I include POSS-*ing* and *that*-clause constructions in the contrast from (29)–(31):

(29)  a. The/John's book
  b. $^{??}$The/$^{??}$John's singing (of) the song  } is red/thin/smooth/dusty.
  c. $^{??}$That John is singing the song

(30) Sally touched/ was looking at
  a. the/John's book
  b. $^{??}$the/$^{??}$John's singing (of) the song
  c. $^{??}$that John was singing the song

(31) Paul pulled/kicked/ tore apart
  a. the/John's book
  b. $^{??}$the/$^{??}$John's singing (of) the song
  c. $^{??}$that John was singing the song

Vendler observes that the above predicates share reference to (points in) space. Since he assumes that individual objects "are in a place, but ... do not take place at a certain time" (Vendler, 1967b, 144), he identifies the denotations of concrete referential DPs with individuals (as opposed to events). The separation of individuals and events is supported by Moltmann's (2020a) work on the ontological import of specific existential constructions. This work has found that different English existence predicates (e.g. *exist*, *occur*, *obtain*) select for semantic arguments from different ontological categories and with different spatial and/or temporal properties:

(32)  a. John's book  
      b. $^{??}$The/$^{??}$John's singing of the song  } exists.  
      c. $^{??}$John's singing the song

(33)  a. $^{??}$John's book  
      b. The/John's singing of the song } occurred/happened/took place  
      c. $^{??}$John's singing the song                                yesterday.

In particular, Moltmann (2020a) observes that, whereas "*exist* [only] applies to material and abstract objects" excluding events and facts (318), *occur* and *obtain* only select for events and, respectively, for facts. This observation warrants an analogous semantic categorization to the one from Vendler (1967a, 1967b). Rett (2022) extends Vendler and Moltmann's strategy by replacing existence predicates by (nominal, adjectival, and adverbial) modifiers (see also Rett, 2018). Such modifiers can be used to distinguish degrees (i.e. the semantic arguments of *very*; see (34a)) from kinds (i.e. the semantic arguments of *endangered*; see (34b)):

(34) Emmy is very { a. tall.  
                    b. $^{??}$Javan rhinos/the Javan rhino.

Their successful distinction of ontological categories suggests that Vendler and Moltmann's strategies can be extended to any selectionally restrictive predicates whatsoever. Such generalization would only exclude selectionally super-flexible predicates like *remember*, which combine with declarative and interrogative finite clauses, infinitival clauses, gerunds, and concrete referential DPs alike (see Liefke, 2021). However, this generalization results in a plethora of ontological categories that much exceed Bach's ontological zoo. An example of such undesirable multiplication of ontological categories is given in (35). In this example, the difference in acceptability between (35a) and (35b/c) seems to indicate an ontological distinction between animate objects (see (35a)) and (concrete or abstract) inanimate objects (see (35b/c)). However, this distinction is not reflected in any mainstream semantic ontologies.

(35) a. Paul's cat/The orchid in my office  
    b. ??The book/??Betty's wedding ring } has genes/will eventually  
    c. ??Pegasus/??Matti's favorite color                              die.

To avoid both a return to an extreme version of Bach's ontological zoo and the assumption of a single ontological category (as suggested by (24)/(25c); but see Liefke & Werning, 2018; Sutton, 2024), it seems advisable to combine the selection-based strategy for the identification of ontological categories with other, different, strategies. One such strategy is presented in Section 2.3. This strategy uses morphological items that are dedicated to a particular semantic category (Rett, 2022; see also Asher, 1993; Moltmann, 2013a). Since this strategy uses the same proform, namely, *it*, for reference to animate and inanimate objects (see (36)), it suggests their ontological co-classification.

(36) a. [Paul's cat]$_i$/[The orchid in my office]$_i$  
    b. [The book]$_i$/[Betty's wedding ring]$_i$ } is beautiful/awesome.  
    c. [Pegasus]$_i$/[Matti's favorite color]$_i$       Mia likes it$_i$.

We will see in the next subsection that the pronoun *it*, in fact, enables reference to a much wider class of objects than just individuals. This is yet more motivation for the suggestion to combine strategies.

## 2.3 The Morphological Strategy: Proforms

I have already mentioned that ontological categories can also be identified through 'morphological category-specific items'. This identification assumes that different such items are used to refer to entities from distinct ontological categories. Morphological category-specific items include quantifiers as well as proforms (paradigmatically, anaphoric pronouns and, on some accounts, *wh*-words). The study of these items is motivated by the assumption that natural languages lexicalize reference to different types of entities. A selection of English proforms, *wh*-words, and quantifiers is given in Table 1 (based on Rett, 2018, 5; see also Rett, 2022, 283–285). This selection includes (among others) individual proforms (e.g. *he*, *she*, *it*; see Bittner, 2001, 2011), temporal proforms (e.g. tense markers; see Partee, 1973, 1984), modal proforms (e.g. *will*, *would*; see Stone, 1997), and propositional/sentential proforms (e.g. *that*; see Moltmann, 2013a; Potts, 2002).[21] The items in Table 1 are surprisingly robust across (unrelated) languages. This holds despite the fact that languages differ

---

[21] For reasons of space, I only list strong quantifiers in Table 1.

**Table 1** Proforms for entities from different semantic categories

| Category | Pronoun | *wh*-word | Quantifier |
|---|---|---|---|
| individuals | he, she, it | who, which, what | all, everything/-one |
| events | it | which, when, what | always, if |
| worlds/situations | will, would, then | ? when (see (42a)) | must, might, if |
| times | then, -ed [past tense morpheme] | when | always, daily, when(ever) |
| locations | there, it | where | everywhere, where(ever) |
| propositions | that, it | what | everything, what(ever) |
| degrees | yea, so | how (many/much) | more, -er |
| manners | (like) so | how | ? like |
| kinds | so, such | how | all |

with respect to which elements they unite lexically (e.g. quantificational force, flavor, or evidential base; see Matthewson, 2010; reported in Rett, 2022, 283).

Importantly, different proforms help disambiguate between different readings of a sentence or sentential constituent (Mery & Retoré, 2017). This holds for the complement in (37), which can be analyzed either as a 'DP + adjunct' construction (in which *swimming* is an optional predicate that modifies the DP *a woman*; see Williams, 1983) or as a gerundive ACC-*ing* construction (in which *a woman swimming* forms a constituent; see D'Ambrosio & Stoljar, 2021). Since the anaphoric pronoun *it* cannot bind the DP *a woman*, (37b) requires the ACC-*ing* reading. Given this reading, (37b) identifies (the event of) the woman's swimming as the cause of Zeno's shiver. Since anaphoric *she* binds the DP *a woman* more easily when the matrix verb, *see*, is interpreted as a transitive verb (such that *swimming* serves as an adjunct), (37a) prefers the 'DP + adjunct' reading.

(37) Zeno saw [[a woman]$_i$ swimming]$_j$.
 a. She$_i$ was wearing a wetsuit.       (individual)
 b. It$_j$ made Zeno shiver.         (event)

Notably, pronouns can also serve in the resolution of semantic ambiguities, for example, of the sentence in (38).[22] In this sentence, the DP *the RMS Queen Mary* can denote either an individual (namely, the ship Queen Mary) or an event (namely, the Queen Mary's passage). In (38a) and (38b), the pronouns *she* and *it* pick out the former and the latter, respectively.

(38) The RMS Queen Mary passed through the sluice last year.
 a. She was as beautiful as ever.       (individual)
 b. It was quite an event.         (event)

A quick glance at Table 1 already reveals that, by themselves, proforms and quantifiers may not be able to distinguish between intuitively different semantic categories. Thus, the anaphoric pronoun *it* can be used to refer to individuals (in (39a)) as well as to events (in (39b)) and propositions (in (39c)) (a similar observation is made in Asher, 1993, 3). The same holds for the *wh*-word *what* (see (40)):

(39) a. Berta baked [a cake]$_i$. Anna ate it$_i$.   (individual)
  b. [The squeaking of the door]$_i$ caused Mia to cringe. It$_i$  (event)
   made Noel's ears hurt.
  c. Ben believes [that figs are fruit]$_i$. Dana doubts it$_i$.  (proposition)

---

[22] The example is inspired by Krifka (1990).

(40) a. Anna ate what/everything (that) Berta baked, namely, a cake.
(individual)

b. What caused Mia to cringe made Noel's ears hurt. (event)

c. Ben believes what Dana doubts, namely, that figs are fruit.
(proposition)

Considerations like these also apply to proforms for other semantic categories. Thus, the German pronoun *so* (roughly translated *such*) is ambiguous between kinds (in (41a)), manners (in (41b)), and degrees (in (41c); see Anderson & Morzycki, 2015, 795; based on Umbach & Ebert, 2009). In English, a parallel behavior is displayed by the complementizer *as* (Anderson & Morzycki, 2015).

(41) a. So einen Hund will ich auch! (kind)
Such a dog want I too.
'I want a dog of this/the same kind.'

b. Berta hat so getanzt. (manner)
Berta has such danced.
'Berta danced like that.'

c. Ich bin so groß. (degree)
I am such tall.
'I am this tall.'

Analogous observations hold for the *wh*-word *when*. The latter can be used to refer to possible worlds (or situations; in (42a)), times (in (42b)), and (possibly) locations:

(42) a. Mary opens the door when(ever) the bell rings. (Rett, 2022, 291)
(situation)

b. When I was young, I had better eyesight. (time)

The data from (39) to (42) support a co-classification – or uniform representation – of individuals and events (Bach, 1986a; Krifka, 1990), of kinds, manners, and degrees (Anderson & Morzycki, 2015; Landman, 2006), and of worlds, times, and locations (Cresswell, 1990; Kratzer, 2019).

The use of a single pronoun for objects from different semantic categories notwithstanding, certain pronouns and *wh*-words still saliently refer to objects from different categories. This is illustrated for the words *what*, *where*, and *when* in (43). These words serve as the *wh*-heads of the nonrestrictive relative clauses that modify the phrases *a pizza*, *in the kitchen*, and *at noon*, respectively:

(43) Fido is eating { a. at noon, when/??where/??what Ella is eating
b. in the kitchen, ??when/where/??what Ella is eating
c. a pizza, namely, ??when/??where/what Ella is eating }.

I have previously focused on the challenge from co-classification, according to which a single proform applies to intuitively distinct semantic categories. In languages with a rich system of pronominal agreement (e.g. Bantu languages), this challenge also has an inverse, namely, categorial multiplicity. In these languages, a single noun can belong to one or more of over a dozen 'genders' (i.e. singular/plural pairings) that are distinguished by pronominal agreement (see, e.g. Marten & Kempson, 2002; McCormack, 2007).[23] When taken at face value, such multi-categorization would yield 'polycentric' (Palmer & Woodman, 2000) or even contradictory semantic categories (see Contini-Morava, 2000; Selvik, 2001).

The observations from the present and the previous subsection suggest that one could distinguish semantic categories by considering the selection- and reference behavior of ALL proforms and quantifiers that are associated with a given semantic category, and by drawing category distinctions on the basis of the most selective of these proforms/quantifiers. This is in line with the assumption (reported in Rett, 2022, 288, and attributed to Partee, 1973, 1984) that a language differentiates between two entities $x$ and $y$ if it lexicalizes different proforms for $x$ and $y$, AND if it lexicalizes different quantifiers over $x$ and $y$.[24]

## 2.4 The Logical-Semantic Strategy: Quantificational Domains

My previous strategies for identifying a language's ontological commitments have focused on different aspects of this language itself (i.e. predicates and their selection behavior, quantifiers and proforms). In semantics and the philosophy of language, these strategies are often (implicitly) complemented by a strategy that focuses on the formal semantic modelling of this language, namely, by a *theory-internal* strategy. This strategy is based on the observation that certain phenomena (paradigmatically: sentential entailments) can only be modelled if we assume an extra semantic domain whose elements are denoted by implicit (syntactic or logical) arguments. I discuss the most salient such domains in Sections 2.4.2 and 2.4.3. To make the assumptions that go into

---

[23] I thank an anonymous reviewer for raising my awareness of this point.
[24] Rett includes the further condition that the language lexicalizes different modifiers of $x$ and $y$. I here exclude this condition for reasons of space.

this modelling explicit, I precede this discussion with a brief description of the adopted interpretation method.[25]

### 2.4.1 The Method: Indirect Interpretation

To obtain linguistic meanings, this Element will use Montague's (1973) method of indirect interpretation. This method obtains the semantic values of natural language expressions indirectly, namely, by interpreting these expressions' logical 'translations' in set-theoretic models (typically: models of some $n$-sorted version, $TY_n$, of Gallin's (1975) higher-order logic $TY_2$). The semantic interpretation of natural language thus proceeds in three steps:

- ❶ analyze the syntax of a non-trivial natural language fragment (here: a fragment of contemporary American English; see Section 2.1.2);
- ❷ develop a language ($\mathcal{L}$), model-theoretic domain ($\mathcal{F}$), and interpretation function ($\mathcal{I}$) for the interpreting logic (here: $TY_n$);
- ❸ provide a translation function, ⤳, (or, historically, a set of translation rules) that sends analyzed linguistic expressions to logical terms.

Figure 2 (adapted from Roelofsen, 2008, 15) illustrates the interpretation, $\mathcal{I}(\chi)$, of a natural language expression $X$ via $X$'s translation into the logical term $\chi$. To prime intuitions, this interpretation is illustrated on the example of the proper name *Brutus* from (44) (see (45)). In this example, **brutus** is an individual $TY_n$ constant that serves as the logical translation of the English proper name *Brutus* (such that *Brutus* ⤳ **brutus**). Its interpretation, that is, [= $\mathcal{I}$(**brutus**)], is an object in the domain of the designated $TY_n$ model.

Since the bulk of arguments for certain ontological categories is independent of the specific elements in the model's domains (see Section 2.4.2–2.4.3 and Section 4), this Element will often stay at the level of logical translations (this level is printed as a darker box with a double frame in Figure 2). This

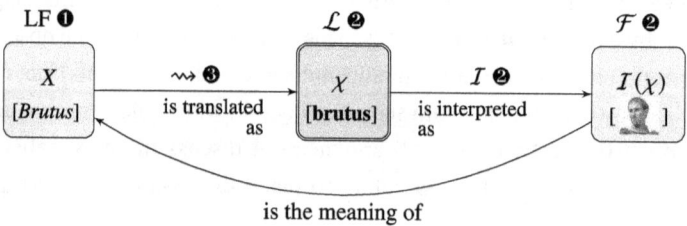

**Figure 2** The method of indirect interpretation.

---

[25] For a more thorough exposition of this method, the reader is referred to Janssen and Zimmermann (2021), section 2.3.

option is not available for semantics like Heim and Kratzer (1998), which interpret natural language expressions into logical models directly, without using an intermediary logical language. In the few instances where it is helpful to stay neutral between these competing approaches (e.g. in Section 1 and in Section 5.2), I introduce linguistic meanings through semantic brackets, $[\![\cdot]\!]$, (such that $[\![X]\!] = \mathcal{I}(\chi)$, where $X \rightsquigarrow \chi$).

My decision to adopt the method of indirect interpretation is motivated by its domain- and language-independence. I have already pointed out that a focus on logical translations obviates the use of specific set-theoretic models. As a result, this strategy avoids false ontological conclusions that may be brought in by our particular choice of model-theoretic domain(s). Since the Quinean strategy for identifying ontological commitments (see Section 2.4.2–2.4.3) is targeted at existentially quantified variables, it fits more squarely with our preferred 'logical language'-based indirect interpretation strategy.

To avoid introducing too much complexity, I will not give a detailed specification of the translation function $\rightsquigarrow$ (see step ❸; Heim & Kratzer, 1998, ch. 3.1; Zimmermann & Sternefeld, 2013).[26] Instead, I will only assume that there is a principled way of translating complex linguistic expressions, which takes into account the logical translations of these expressions' syntactic constituents.

To ease the reader into Quine's strategy for identifying ontological commitments, I finish this subsection by surveying our 'intermediate' logical language, $\mathcal{L}$: This language assumes a fixed stock of variables and nonlogical constants. From these basic expressions, it obtains complex terms inductively through the usual connectives (i.e. $=, \neg, \wedge, \vee, \rightarrow$) and quantifiers ($\forall, \exists$), as well as through F(unctional) A(pplication) and lambda abstraction (for the denotation of functions). In virtue of FA, the application of a function term, $\boldsymbol{B}$, to a (suitably typed) argument term, $\boldsymbol{A}$, i.e. $\boldsymbol{B}(\boldsymbol{A})$, is also a TY term.[27] In particular, in (45a–c), functional application allows us to build an open formula, **brutal**($e$), from the function term **brutal** (which denotes the functional equivalent of a property of events) and the event variable $e$. In the next section, nonlogical constants (e.g. **brutal**) are given bold print. Variables (e.g. $e$ [event], $x$ [individual], and $w$ [possible world]) are written in italics.

---

[26] The interested reader is referred to Klein and Sag (1985).
[27] The same holds for the result, $\lambda x. A$, of abstracting over the argument of a $TY_n$ term $A$. This result denotes a function whose application to some argument $d$ (that must have the same type as $x$) returns the value of $A$ with $x$ interpreted as $d$. To avoid unnecessary complexity, most of this Element will use logical translations of full declarative sentences (i.e. formulas), and will only silently assume that these formulas are compositionally obtained from structured natural language input. Keep in mind, however, that a fully compositional interpretation is, at least in principle, possible for all discussed examples.

### 2.4.2 Events

I have shown in Sections 2.2 and 2.3 that events serve as the intuitive referents of nominal gerunds and of certain proforms and quantifiers. A commitment to events is further supported by the observation that we need events to account for entailments like (44). These entailments are based on different instances of modifier-dropping (see (44a–d), due to Parsons, 1972; cf. Colapinto, 2020). Because of their particular visual shape, these entailments are sometimes called 'diamond entailments' (Wyner, 1994; see also Landman, 2000).

(44)  a. Brutus brutally stabbed Caesar on the forum at noon.
  ⇒ b. Brutus brutally stabbed Caesar on the forum.  (temporal-PP drop)
  ⇒ c. Brutus brutally stabbed Caesar.  (locative-PP drop)
  ⇒ d. Brutus stabbed Caesar.  (adverb drop)

Davidson (2001) has pointed out that, by interpreting verbs like *stab* in (44) as relations between events and their arguments, one can straightforwardly account for these entailments (namely, through conjunction elimination, as illustrated by the logical translations of (44a–d) in (45)).[28] On his account, action verbs like *stab* have an additional argument slot for events. Adverbs like *brutally* are interpreted as properties of events. In (45), $e$ is a variable over events. '**stabbing**$(e, \textbf{brutus}, \textbf{caesar})$' expresses that $e$ is a stabbing event by Brutus whose object (or 'theme') is Caesar.[29] The functions **loc** (for 'location') and **time** (for 'point in time') describe the particular ways in which entities take part in an event.

(45)  a. $(\exists e)[\textbf{stab}(e, \textbf{brutus}, \textbf{caesar}) \wedge \textbf{brutal}(e) \wedge \textbf{loc}(e) = \textbf{forum} \wedge \textbf{time}(e) = \textbf{noon}]$
  b. $(\exists e)[\textbf{stab}(e, \textbf{brutus}, \textbf{caesar}) \wedge \textbf{brutal}(e) \wedge \textbf{loc}(e) = \textbf{forum}]$
  c. $(\exists e)[\textbf{stab}(e, \textbf{brutus}, \textbf{caesar}) \wedge \textbf{brutal}(e)]$
  d. $(\exists e)[\textbf{stab}(e, \textbf{brutus}, \textbf{caesar})]$

Since (45a–d) involve existential quantification over events, Davidson's argument for events is close in spirit to Quine's (1948) criterion of ontological commitment. This criterion assumes that "to be is ... to be the value of a

---

[28] Since the classical Davidsonian account of action sentences distinguishes between arguments and adjuncts, I here adopt this account. The alternative neo-Davidsonian account analyzes (44a) as $(\exists e)[\textbf{ag}(e, \textbf{brutus}) \wedge \textbf{stab}(e) \wedge \textbf{th}(e, \textbf{caesar}) \wedge \textbf{loc}(e, \textbf{forum}) \wedge \textbf{time}(e, \textbf{noon})]$, where **ag** and **th** are the thematic roles 'agent' and 'theme'.

[29] In all formulas in the rest of this Element, I follow the convention that a function's simultaneous application to a sequence of arguments indicates successive application in the reverse order of the arguments. This strategy is commonly called 'Currying' (following Curry, 1961), or 'Schönfinkelization' (following Schönfinkel, 1924; see Heim & Kratzer, 1998, 30–31).

variable" (Quine, 1948, 32), that is, to lie in the domain of (existential) quantification. Davidson acknowledges this connection to Quine when he remarks that "ontology is forced into the open only where the theory finds quantificational structure" (Davidson, 1977, 251).

The semantic commitment to events is further supported by the observation that existential quantification over events is required to account for the possibility of permuting adverbial modifiers (in (46): *slowly* and *with a stick*; see Landman, 2000; Moltmann, 2007). It further accounts for the reference of anaphoric pronouns in sentences like (47) (Davidson, 2001; see Asher 2003; Colapinto, 2020), for the interpretation of aspect (in (48); see Kratzer, 1998), and for the intuitive truth- and entailment-conditions of experiential attitude reports (e.g. (49)–(50); see Higginbotham, 1983, 2003; cf. Stephenson, 2010). In particular, unlike its *that*-clause counterpart, (50) is false in a scenario in which John has only been told that Mary was singing, but has not himself heard Mary sing. In (46b), '**instr**(*e*)' identifies the instrument that is used to perform the event *e*.

(46) a. John walked slowly with a stick. (Moltmann, 2007, 377, ex. (19))
≡ b. John walked with a stick slowly.
⤳ $(\exists e)[\textbf{walk}(e, \textbf{john}) \wedge \textbf{slow}(e) \wedge \textbf{instr}(e) = \textbf{stick}]$

(47) Ben fell (down the stairs). It happened at his workplace.
⤳ $(\exists e)[\textbf{fall}(e, \textbf{ben}) \wedge \textbf{loc}(e) = \textbf{ben's-workplace}]$

(48) Ralph is running.
⤳ $\lambda t (\exists e)[t \subseteq \textbf{time}(e) \wedge \textbf{run}(e, \textbf{ralph})]$

(49) a. John saw Mary leave.
⤳ $(\exists e)[\textbf{leave}(e, \textbf{mary}) \wedge \textbf{see}(\textbf{john}, e)]$
⇒ b. Mary left. (Higginbotham, 1983, 106–107)
⤳ $(\exists e)[\textbf{leave}(e, \textbf{mary})]$

(50) John remembers Mary singing. (Higginbotham, 2003, 505)
(≢ John remembers that Mary was singing.)
⤳ $(\exists e)[\textbf{sing}(e, \textbf{mary}) \wedge (\exists e')[\textbf{remember}(e', \textbf{John}, e)]]$

### 2.4.3 Possible Worlds

It is commonly assumed that an adequate treatment of modal expressions (e.g. auxiliaries like *must* or *have to*, and adverbs like *necessarily* or *certainly*) involves quantification over possible worlds (see Knuuttila, 2003, who traces this idea back to medieval philosophy and to Leibniz). Following Hintikka

(1957) and Kripke (1959), nearly all contemporary semantic theories interpret modals through existential quantification (in the case of weak modals like *may*) or universal quantification over worlds (in the case of strong modals like *must*).[30] A simple semantics that captures this idea is given in (51) (see Montague, 1970).

(51)    a.   It may be raining in Bochum.   ⤳   $(\exists w)[\mathbf{rain}(w, \mathbf{bochum})]$
         b.   It must be raining in Bochum.   ⤳   $(\forall w)[\mathbf{rain}(w, \mathbf{bochum})]$

State-of-the-art semantics for modal expressions (which account for different flavors of modality, e.g. epistemic, deontic) likewise involve quantification over possible worlds. In these semantics (exemplified in (52), based on von Fintel & Heim, 2021; see Kratzer, 1991), $f$ is a 'flavor' function that projects a set of possible worlds from the anchor of the modal claim, $w$.

(52)    a.   It may be raining in Bochum.
           ⤳   $(\exists w')[f(w)(w') \wedge \mathbf{rain}(w', \mathbf{bochum})]$
         b.   It must be raining in Bochum.
           ⤳   $(\forall w')[f(w)(w') \rightarrow \mathbf{rain}(w', \mathbf{bochum})]$

Like modals, propositional attitude predicates (e.g. *believe*, *want*) are often also interpreted as involving possible worlds (following Hintikka, 1969; Montague, 1970, 1973). Intuitively, these predicates express relations between an individual agent (i.e. the semantic value of the predicate's grammatical subject) and propositions/sets of possible worlds (i.e. the semantic value of the predicate's complement; see Russell, 1905). The familiar semantics for these predicates (due to Hintikka, 1969; see von Fintel & Heim, 2021; Stalnaker, 1978) involves partitioning the set of possible worlds into worlds (i.e. the agent's attitudinal alternatives) that are compatible with the agent's attitude and worlds that are incompatible with this attitude. It interprets the attitude predicate as a universal quantifier over the agent's attitudinal alternatives. For the attitude report in (53a), the resulting semantics is given in (53b), where $\mathrm{DOX}_{\mathbf{bert},@}$ is the set of Bert's doxastic [= belief-]alternatives in the actual world, @.

(53)    a.   Bert believes that Suzy is smart.
        ⤳   b.   $\lambda p \lambda x (\forall w)[\mathrm{DOX}_{x,@}(w) \rightarrow p(w)](\mathbf{bert}, \lambda w'.\mathbf{smart}(w', \mathbf{suzy}))$
             $\equiv (\forall w)[\mathrm{DOX}_{\mathbf{bert},@}(w) \rightarrow \mathbf{smart}(w, \mathbf{suzy})]$

---

[30] An exception is Thomason's (1980) Intentional Logic (IntL) (see Muskens, 2005), which interprets modal adverbs like *necessarily* as functions over semantically primitive propositions. However, since IntL assumes a surjective map from primitive propositions to sets of possible worlds, it is debatable whether this logic is truly 'world-free'.

The interpretation of attitude complements in terms of lambda abstraction over possible worlds (i.e. as sets of worlds; see the second line in (53a)) enables the modelling of entailment as set-theoretic inclusion (see Liefke, 2024; Sinhababu, 2015). On this account, a sentence $X$ entails another sentence, $Y$, i.e. $X \Rightarrow Y$, iff $[\![X]\!] \subseteq [\![Y]\!]$ (Kac, 1992; Keenan & Faltz, 1985). This relation is exemplified by the sentences in (54):

(54)    a.   Suzy is smart and hardworking.
          ⤳ $\lambda w'.\,\mathbf{smart}(w', \mathbf{suzy}) \wedge \mathbf{hardworking}(w', \mathbf{suzy})$

$\Rightarrow$   b.   Suzy is smart.
          ⤳ $\lambda w'.\,\mathbf{smart}(w', \mathbf{suzy})$

Assuming that *believe* is upward monotonic in its complement position (such that, for all $p \subseteq q$, any agent who believes $p$ will also believe $q$),[31] this account straightforwardly captures the validity of the inference in (55):

(55)    a.   Bert believes that Suzy is smart and hardworking.
          ⤳ $\lambda p \lambda x (\forall w)[\mathrm{DOX}_{x,@}(w) \to p(w)](\lambda w'.\,\mathbf{smart}(w', \mathbf{suzy}) \wedge$
                                    $\mathbf{hardworking}(w', \mathbf{suzy}))(\mathbf{bert})$

$\Rightarrow$   b.   Bert believes that Suzy is smart.
          ⤳ $\lambda p \lambda x (\forall w)[\mathrm{DOX}_{x,@}(w) \to p(w)](\lambda w'.\,\mathbf{smart}(w', \mathbf{suzy}))(\mathbf{bert})$

Abstracting over possible worlds also enables a uniform account of (propositional and objectual) intensionality, as I have shown in Liefke (2024) (see Montague, 2007).

## 2.5 Example-Based Comparison of the Different Strategies

The strategies from the previous subsections identify the ontological categories of natural language semantics with (i) the semantic arguments of predicates that have same semantic selection properties, with (ii) the referents of proforms, and with (iii) the domains of quantification in formal-semantic analyses. In quite a few cases, the different strategies agree in their judgments. This holds, for example, for the distinction between individuals and propositions. In particular, the expressions that denote these different entities (in (56): the DP *Bob's sister*

---

[31] Its usefulness in validating (54) notwithstanding, the upward monotonicity of *believe* (and of other representational attitude) complements is highly controversial. This holds especially since the combination of monotonicity with a possible worlds-account of intensionality makes counterintuitive predictions about the agent's beliefs (including the agent's 'logical omniscience', see Hintikka, 1962; cf. Barwise & Perry, 1983; Cresswell, 1973; Lewis, 1972). These predictions have been a driving force behind alternative approaches to intensional and attitude contents, like Barwise/Perry (1983)-style situation semantics and hyperintensional semantics (see e.g. Pollard, 2015; Thomason, 1980).

and the CP *that someone teased Bob's sister*) are not only licensed by different predicates (here: by the emotion adjective *annoyed* and, respectively, by the modal adjective *likely*; see (57)). They are also picked up by different anaphoric pronouns (here: by the proforms *her* resp. *it*). For the example in (56), the individual/proposition distinction is thus supported by the selection-based strategy from Section 2.2 as well as by the proform-based strategy from Section 2.3.

(56) a. [Bob's sister]$_i$ is annoyed. Someone teased her$_i$/$^{??}$it$_i$.

b. [That someone teased Bob's sister]$_i$ is likely. But Bob doesn't believe it$_i$/$^?$her$_i$.

(57) a. $^{??}$[That someone teased Bob's sister]$_i$ is annoyed.

b. $^{??}$[Bob's sister]$_i$ is likely.

The success of these strategies is challenged by the observation that their judgements diverge for certain other categories. Problematic categories of this sort include events and facts. Intuitively, the sentences in (58) resist substituting their subject (here: the nominal gerund *John's singing of the song* or the verbal gerund *John's singing the song*) by the subject of the other sentence. The deviance of (59a) and (59b) suggests that *John's singing of the song* belongs to a different semantic category than *John's singing the song*. However, both constructions can serve as the anaphoric antecedents of the pronoun *it* (see the second sentence in (58a/b)). While the proform-based strategy from Section 2.3 thus predicts a co-categorization of ⟦John's singing of the song⟧ and ⟦John's singing the song⟧ (possibly in the category of Kratzerian situations; see Kratzer, 2002, 2019), the selection-based strategy from Section 2.2 predicts their classification in *different* semantic categories, namely, as events respectively as facts.

(58) a. [John's singing of the song]$_i$ was loud. It$_i$ woke the sleeping dog.

b. [John's singing the song]$_i$ made Mia blush. She had not expected it$_i$.

(59) a. $^{??}$John's singing the song was loud.

b. $^?$John's singing of the song made Mia blush.

The above-described tension also holds for judgments about manners, degrees, and kinds: While the German expressions *Hund* ['dog'], *getanzt* ['danced'], and *groß* ['tall'] in (60) combine with different modifiers (i.e. *selten* ['rare'], *schwungvoll* ['spiritedly'], or *1.80m* [1.80 meters]) and are analyzed through quantification – or abstraction – over different domains (i.e. kinds $k$, manners $m$, and degrees $d$; see the interpretation of the respective second sentence in each of (60a–c), in (61a-c)),[32] they are still picked up by the same anaphoric pronoun, *so*. Regarding a co-categorization of manners, degrees, and kinds, the judgments of the proform-based strategy thus conflict with the judgments of the selection- and quantification-based strategies.

(60) a. Frank besitzt einen [seltenen]$_i$ Hund. Fred besitzt auch so$_i$ einen Hund.
Frank owns a rare dog. Fred owns also such a dog.
'Frank owns a dog of a rare breed. Fred owns a dog of this/the same kind.'

b. Susi hat [schwungvoll]$_i$ getanzt. Hans hat auch so$_i$ getanzt.
Susi has spiritedly danced. Hans has also such danced.
'Susi was dancing spiritedly. Hans was dancing in the same way/manner.'

c. Berta ist [1.80m]$_i$ groß. Anna ist auch so$_i$ groß.
(Umbach & Gust, 2014, 76, (2))
Berta is 1.80m tall. Anna is also such tall.
'Berta is 1.80m tall. Anne is that tall, too.'

(61) a. (60a) ⤳ $(\exists x)[(\mathbf{dog}(x) \wedge \mathbf{own}(\mathbf{fred},x)) \wedge (\exists k)[x \leq k \wedge \mathbf{rare}(k)]]$

b. (60b) ⤳ $(\exists e)[\mathbf{dance}(e,\mathbf{hans}) \wedge (\exists m)[\mathbf{manner}(m,e) \wedge \mathbf{spirited}(m)]]$

c. (60c) ⤳ $\mathbf{max}(\lambda d.\, \mu_{\text{height}}(\mathbf{anna}) \geq d) = 1.80$

Some researchers have interpreted this conflict as support for unifying the categories of manners, degrees, and kinds (see e.g. Anderson & Morzycki, 2015; Moltmann, 2009). However, instead of describing the details of such unification (for which the interested reader is referred to the cited original works), I directly apply the above strategies to different fragments and languages.

## 3 Montague's Semantic Ontology

The previous sections have already suggested that differences in a language's vocabulary (e.g. whether or not [a certain fragment of] a language contains tense markers or degree expressions) may have an effect on the semantic categories in the language's ontology. This is indeed the case, as is evidenced by the ontology of Montague's fragment from "The proper treatment of quantification

---

[32] The interpretation in (61a) is based on Carlson (1977, 370–380) and Landman (2006, 45–70). In this interpretation, $\leq$ is the instantiation relation between individuals and kinds.

in ordinary English" (1973) (hereafter, the 'PTQ-fragment' – or simply, 'PTQ'). The PTQ-fragment is a proper part of English that excludes measure phrases, degree modifiers, and explicit comparatives alongside modifiers for kinds and interrogative expressions. As a result of the former, PTQ's ontology is similar to the ontology of what have been argued to be 'degree-less' languages like Motu (Beck et al., 2009) and Washo (Bochnak, 2015) (see Section 4.5). As a result of the latter, PTQ's ontology lacks kinds and questions. Since Montague assumes that an adequate interpretation of expressions like *the event of the sun's rising* does not require events (see my discussion surrounding (10) in Section 2.1.1), his ontology – expectedly – also does not include events.

In Section 3, I will first provide a more detailed presentation of the PTQ-fragment and its semantic ontology. Since this fragment is a very small, well-defined subset of Montague's local variety of 1970's English with a fully specified ontology, it provides the perfect object for our study. The ontology of this fragment is supported by a combination of the strategies from Section 2. In particular, the morphological and the lexical-semantic strategy both support the commitment of this fragment (or its logical translation) to individuals. The lexical strategy supports its commitment to propositions and (first- and higher-order) properties.

Montague intended the PTQ-ontology to provide a semantic explanation for grammaticality and ungrammaticality (but see my remarks in Section 5.2).[33] To make this possible, his ontology has baked in all syntactically relevant semantic distinctions (esp. individual vs. proposition, individual vs. property vs. quantifier). In Section 4, I will describe extensions of the PTQ-ontology to semantic ontologies for richer fragments of English and other languages along the lines of Sections 2.4.2 and 2.4.3. I will further contrast global [= universal/cross-linguistically robust] with local [= fragment-/language-specific] semantic ontologies.

To facilitate a structured presentation of PTQ's ontology – and to limit the effects of Montague's strategy of 'generalizing to the worst case' (see Section 2.1.2) – I divide the PTQ-fragment into an extensional and an intensional part. The extensional part (in Table 2) is that part of the fragment whose expressions allow the truth-preserving substitution of co-referential expressions (e.g. *Jocasta, Oedipus' mother*) and truth-conditional equivalents (e.g. *Oedipus married Jocasta, Oedipus married his mother*; see (27) in Section 2.2.3).[34] In virtue of this substitutivity, the extensional part of the

---

[33] This also stands in contrast to the observation (discussed in Section 2.1.2) that this strategy famously fails to capture the distributional difference between common nouns and intransitive verbs.

[34] For a more sophisticated characterization of intensionality (which treats intensionality as a complex disjunctive property that comprises referential opacity, non-specificity, and lack of existential commitment), the reader is referred to Forbes (2006) and Zimmermann (2001).

**Table 2** The extensional part of Montague's PTQ-fragment

| | | |
|---|---|---|
| pronouns: | $he_0, he_1, he_2, \ldots$ | (individuals) |
| proper names: | *John, Mary, Bill* | (GQ's) |
| decl. sentences: | *John walks*, ... | (truth-values) |
| common nouns: | *man, woman, park, fish, pen* | (properties of individuals) |
| intrans. verbs: | *run, walk, talk* | (properties of individuals) |
| transitive verbs: | *find, lose, eat, date, be* | (relations betw. individ'ls) |
| adverbs: | *rapidly, slowly* | (relations betw. properties) |
| determiners: | *a, the* | (property/GQ-relations) |
| quantifiers: | *every* | (property/GQ-relations) |
| prepositions: | *in* | (...) |

PTQ-fragment lets proper names be interpreted as individuals (represented by properties of properties of individuals [= 'generalized quantifiers']) – rather than as individual concepts (or their representing properties of properties of individual concepts).[35] Analogous observations hold for the interpretation of nouns and intransitive verbs as properties of individuals (rather than as properties of individual concepts; see Zimmermann, 2022, 341–342). Table 2 includes the expressions' semantic categories in the rightmost column. In this column, 'GQ' is short for 'generalized quantifier'.

In contrast to the elements in Table 2, expressions from the intensional part of the PTQ-fragment (in Table 3) resist the truth-preserving substitution of co-referential or truth-conditionally equivalent expressions (see (26)). Since substitution-resistance is also exemplified by modal contexts, I take the intensional part to include modal expressions (here: the sentence adverb *necessarily*).

Admittedly, it is somewhat odd to present Montague's semantic ontology without simultaneously typing its objects (for example, assigning third person singular pronouns (*he*) the type $e$ [for individuals] and declarative sentences the type $\langle s, t \rangle$ [for propositions, analyzed as sets of possible worlds]). However, to preserve our focus on strategies for identifying a language's (or fragment's) semantic commitments – and in line with this Element's concern with descriptive natural language ontology – I will suppress type assignments. The project of typing the PTQ-ontology will be the central topic of the sequel to this Element, entitled *Reduction and Unification in Natural Language Ontology*.

---

[35] This is justified by the interpretation of proper names as rigid designators [= constant functions from possible worlds to individuals], and by the existence of a one-to-one correspondence between rigid designators and individuals.

**Table 3** The intensional part of Montague's PTQ-fragment

| | | |
|---|---|---|
| declarative complements: | *that ..., to ...[inf.]* | (propositions) |
| sentence adverbs: | *necessarily* | (proposition/truth-value relations) |
| intensional nouns: | *unicorn, price, temperature* | (properties of individual concepts) |
| intransitive verbs: | *rise, change* | (properties of individual concepts) |
| transitive verbs: | *seek* [= *try to find*] | (relations to a centered proposition) |
| clause-taking Vs: | *believe, assert* | (relations to a proposition) |
| control verbs: | *try, wish* | (relations to a centered proposition) |
| adverbs: | *allegedly* | (relations between properties) |
| prepositions: | *about* | (...) |

## 3.1 Montague's Extensional Ontology

The inclusion of individual proforms (e.g. indexed versions of the pronoun *he* in Table 2; see also (62)) already suggests that the PTQ-fragment carries a semantic commitment to individuals. The presence of an individual domain, $A$, in Montague's models supports this suggestion. While Montague's strategy of 'generalizing to the worst case' prevents him from using individuals as the semantic values of referential determiner phrases (DPs), individuals play a central role in his interpretation of determiners and quantifiers (namely, as objects in the domain of existential and universal quantification; see (63), due to Montague, 1973, 266).[36] Montague's interpretation of quantifier phrases and definite/indefinite DPs (in (63): *every man, a/the man*; cf. Russell, 1905) thus reflects the Quinean criterion of ontological commitment (see Section 2.4).

(62)  Every man loves a woman such that she loves him.

(Montague, 1973, 253)

(63)  a.  A man walks. ⇝ $(\exists x)[\mathbf{man}(x) \wedge \mathbf{walk}(x)]$

(Montague, 1973, 253)

   b.  Every man walks. ⇝ $(\forall x)[\mathbf{man}(x) \rightarrow \mathbf{walk}(x)]$

   c.  The man walks. ⇝ $(\exists x)[(\forall y)(\mathbf{man}(y) \leftrightarrow y = x) \wedge \mathbf{walk}(x)]$

Interestingly, in addition to the individual domain $A$, Montague's models also contain a domain, $J$, of points of time. This holds although the PTQ-fragment does not extend to tense or aspectual morphology. (Rather, it only uses times – or, more accurately, ordered world/time pairs – to serve as indices of evaluation; see Section 3.2.) Since Montague further assumes a simple ordering, $\leq$, on $J \times J$ (Montague, 1973, 257–258; see Bach, 1986b, 577), PTQ's ontology allows for a straightforward extension to tense and temporal expressions (along the lines described in (80) in Section 4.2.3; see Partee, 1973, 1984).

## 3.2 Montague's Intensional Ontology

I have already mentioned that possible worlds (i.e. members of Montague's domain $I$) combine with moments of time to yield evaluation indices. While quantification over possible worlds is not overt in Montague's semantics, the modal box operator □ – which is central to Montague's interpretation of the

---

[36] For reasons of readability and coherence, I replace Montague's Polish notation by the more standard infix notation.

sentence adverb *necessarily* – is analyzed in terms of universal quantification over worlds (see (64); Muskens, 1995, 37).[37]

(64)  Necessarily $p \rightsquigarrow \Box p \quad (\equiv \forall w. p(w))$

Possible worlds further play a role in Montague's analysis of the intensional operators $^\vee$ (read: 'cup') and $^\wedge$ (read: 'cap'). The latter correspond to application to and abstraction from the implicit index parameter (see (65), where $\alpha$ is a well-formed expression and $i$ a fixed variable for the evaluation index).

(65)  a.  $^\vee\alpha = \alpha(i)$
      b.  $^\wedge\alpha = \lambda i. \alpha$

Abstraction over possible worlds, $\lambda w$, is instrumental in the complements of finite clause-taking verbs like *believe*, whose complements are commonly interpreted as propositions, analyzed as (characteristic functions of) sets of possible worlds (see the discussion surrounding (69) at the end of this subsection).

To block intuitively invalid inferences like (66) (Montague, 1973, 267–268; attributed to Barbara Partee), Montague interprets some expressions (including the noun *temperature* and the intransitive verb *rise*) as properties of individual concepts. Individual concepts are functions from evaluation indices to individuals. Typically, these functions yield different (numerical) values for different index arguments (as is the case for the DP *the temperature*). However, in special cases (like the intensional interpretation of *ninety*, which allows a reduction to properties of individuals), these functions yield the same value for all arguments (i.e. *ninety* $\rightsquigarrow \lambda i.$ **ninety**; Montague, 1973, 263, postulate (1)). The non-identity of the semantic values of the DPs *the temperature* and *ninety* – and the attendant inability to substitute *the temperature* by *ninety* in (66b) – then blocks the inference to (66c).

(66)  a.  The temperature is ninety.
      b.  The temperature rises.
 $\not\Rightarrow$ c.  $^{??}$Ninety rises.

Montague's argument for the introduction of individual concepts notwithstanding, Kaplan (1976), Muskens (1995), and Liefke and Sanders (2016) have shown that a solution to the temperature puzzle does not require individual concepts. Kaplan maintains the spirit of Montague's solution by replacing individual concepts $c$ by properties of individuals $\lambda x \lambda i. x = c(i)$ (i.e. by Russellian

---

[37] Note that, since Montague identifies indices with ordered world/time-pairs, $\Box \varphi$ correctly abbreviates $\forall \langle w, t \rangle. \varphi$ (read: 'necessarily always $\varphi$'; see Köpping & Zimmermann, 2020, 174). While it is possible to quantify over $w$ and $t$ separately, I here ignore this complication.

(1996) propositional functions). Intensional nouns and intransitive verbs are then interpreted as properties of propositional functions.

Liefke and Sanders solve the temperature puzzle without recourse to intensions altogether. They achieve this by representing the semantic value of *the temperature* in (66b) as a coded sequence of natural numbers (which is itself a natural number) and by approximating the continuous functional that is denoted by *rise* by a lower-type representation of this functional (see Longley & Normann, 2015, ch. 2.3.1). The non-identity of the natural number which codes the *temperature*-sequence and the denotation of *ninety* then blocks the inference in (66). A yet different solution to the temperature puzzle, which uses a modern type-theoretic version of Fillmore's (1982) notion of frame, is given in (Cooper, 2023, ch. 5).

Interestingly, although the PTQ-fragment includes intensional transitive verbs like *seek*, PTQ's ontology does not need to assume relations between individuals and generalized quantifiers. This is a consequence of Montague's lexical decomposition of *seek* as *try to find* (along the lines of Quine, 1956). Montague's interpretation of control verbs like *try* as relations to properties is then inherited down to intensional transitives. In particular, Montague's interpretation of the *de dicto*-reading of (67a) is given in (67b):

(67) a. John seeks a unicorn. (Montague, 1973, 266)

b. John tries [that [$\lambda y_1$. PRO$_1$ finds a unicorn]]
 $\leadsto$ **try-to**$(@, \textbf{john}, \lambda i \lambda y \exists x. \textbf{unicorn}(i,x) \wedge \textbf{find}(i,y,x))$

Zimmermann (2006a) has given an alternative, PTQ-inspired, semantics for (67a) that replaces propositions by properties as the complements of intensional transitive verbs. Zimmermann's semantics has a number of advantages over (67b), including overt compositionality, the ability to account for missing *de dicto*-readings of reports with a strong quantificational object DP (like *each/every/all unicorn(s)*; Zimmermann, 1993), and the ability to avoid inferences to a common objective. In the Zimmermann-style interpretation of (67a) (in (68)), '$P \sqsubseteq$ **unicorn**' asserts that $P$ is an at least equally specific property as the property of being a unicorn.

(68) $(\exists P)[P \sqsubseteq \textbf{unicorn} \wedge \textbf{seek}(i, \textbf{john}, P)]$

Since Zimmermann's semantics involves existential quantification over properties, adopting this semantics would still entail a commitment to properties.

A semantic commitment to properties – or to propositions – would also be brought about by higher-order quantifiers like *what(-ever)* (see Moltmann, 2003; cf. Zimmermann, 2006a). In particular, *what* in (69) is intuitively interpreted as an existential quantifier over propositions $p$ (in (69a)) or over properties $P$ (in (69b)).

(69) a. John believes/asserts what Bill believes, namely, that Mary talks.
⇝ $(\exists p)[\textbf{believe}(\langle @, \textbf{john}, p \rangle) \wedge \textbf{believe}(\langle @, \textbf{bill}, p \rangle) \wedge$
$p = (\lambda i.\, \textbf{talks}(i, \textbf{mary}))]$

b. Mary is seeking what Bill is seeking, namely, a unicorn.
⇝ $(\exists P)[\textbf{try-to}(\langle @, \textbf{mary}, \lambda i \lambda y\, \exists x.\, P(i,x) \wedge \textbf{find}(i,y,x) \rangle) \wedge$
$\textbf{try-to}(\langle @, \textbf{bill}, \lambda i \lambda z\, \exists u.\, P(i,u) \wedge \textbf{find}(i,z,u) \rangle) \wedge$
$P = \textbf{unicorn}]$

## 4 Larger Semantic Ontologies

My discussion so far has suggested that individuals, possible worlds, points of time, propositions, and properties are the common categories of Montague's ontology and the ontology from Section 2. Expectedly, the indicators for semantic commitments from Section 2 (i.e. semantic selection, proforms, and quantificational analyses) also provide support for a series of extensions of the ontology from PTQ. To avoid duplicating my earlier observations, I concentrate on those possible changes to the PTQ-ontology that are triggered by the inadequacy of Montague's own account (see Section 4.1) and that I have hitherto omitted (see Sections 4.2–4.3). Section 4.4 identifies a somewhat surprising possible change (namely, dropping individuals) that goes against what is assumed in Montague's ontology and in many contemporary semantic ontologies.

### 4.1 An Inadequacy-Based Extension: Events

I have already pointed out in my discussion of (10) and at the beginning of Section 3 that Montague (1969) rejects a semantic category of events. While some (!) of the diamond entailments from Section 2.4.2 can indeed be captured without reference to – or quantification over – events (see the Montague-style account of the entailment in (70), where $t$ is a variable over points in time), others require an eventive analysis. This holds, for example, for entailments from sentences with extensional verbs and local prepositional modifiers, see (71):

(70) a. The sun rose at eight. ⇝ $\textbf{rise}(\langle @, \textbf{08:00} \rangle, \textbf{sun})$
⇒ b. The sun rose. ⇝ $(\exists t)[\textbf{rise}(\langle @, t \rangle, \textbf{sun})]$

(71) a. John meets a woman in Paris.
⇝ $\textbf{in}(\lambda y\, \exists x.\, \textbf{woman}(x) \wedge \textbf{meet}(y,x), \textbf{paris})(\textbf{john})$

$\not\Rightarrow$ b. John meets a woman.
$\leadsto (\exists x)[\mathbf{woman}(x) \wedge \mathbf{meet}(\mathbf{john},x)]$

Since the semantics of *in* makes its own structural contribution (as is apparent from (71a)), existentially quantifying over the argument place of **paris** (analogously to (70b); see (72)) does not suffice to validate the entailment in (71) (Zimmermann, 2022, 358–359).

(72) John meets a woman.
$\not\leadsto (\exists z)[\mathbf{in}(\lambda y \exists x. \mathbf{woman}(x) \wedge \mathbf{meet}(y,x), z)(\mathbf{john})]$

To capture the inference in (71), Zimmermann (2022) has proposed to supplement Montague's restrictions on admissible models by a veridicality postulate and a scope principle. The veridicality postulate ensures that "what is done in a specific place (by a specific individual) is done *simpliciter* (by that individual)" (Zimmermann, 2022, 359). The scope principle requires that the quantificational object of an extensional verb takes wide scope with respect to the referential local PP that modifies it (see (73); Zimmermann, 2022, 359). However, as Zimmermann points out (for details, see Zimmermann, 1987; based on Engesser, 1980), the combination of these principles counterintuitively implies that the modifier *in Paris* is redundant in (71a).

(73) a. John meets a woman in Paris.
$\leadsto \mathbf{in}(\lambda y \exists x. \mathbf{woman}(x) \wedge \mathbf{meet}(y,x), \mathbf{paris})(\mathbf{john})$
$\not\Rightarrow$ b. There is a (specific) woman whom John meets in Paris.
$\leadsto (\exists x)[\mathbf{woman}(x) \wedge \mathbf{in}(\lambda y. \mathbf{meet}(y,x), \mathbf{paris})(\mathbf{john})]$

Since an event-semantic account of sentences with prepositional modifiers can straightforwardly capture the entailment behavior in (71) and (73) (see Section 2.4.2), even the PTQ-fragment already requires events.

## 4.2 Coverage-Based Extensions I: Manners, Degrees, and Times

Predictably, to provide an adequate treatment of larger fragments of English, one needs to extend Montague's ontology by those entities (or semantic categories) to which the strategies from Section 2 identify an ontological commitment. This holds, for example, for degrees (which are needed to interpret measure phrases, degree modifiers, and explicit comparatives; see e.g. Cresswell, 1976), manners (which are needed to interpret manner adverbs and *how*-phrases; see e.g. Dik, 1975), and times (which are needed to interpret tense morphemes and to explain tense-related semantic restrictions; see e.g. Partee, 1973). It further holds for pluralities (which are needed to interpret plurals and mass nouns; see Link, 1983), for vectors (which, it has been argued, are needed to interpret locative prepositional phrases; see Zwarts, 1997), and for content individuals (which are needed to interpret content DPs; see Kratzer, 2006).

Below, I will first provide a more detailed argument for the assumption of manners, degrees, and times (in the present subsection) and of pluralities, vectors, and content individuals (in Section 4.3). The addition of further categories (e.g. kinds, situations, and questions) will be postponed to the sequel Element, where these categories (together with the categories from this Element) receive a type-theoretic analysis.

### 4.2.1 Manners

Some researchers have argued that Quine-style quantificational evidence like that from Section 2.4 can also be used to support a semantic commitment to manners. Specifically, the assumption of manners is supported by the observation that the uniform interpretation of adverbs as properties of events (along the lines of Davidson, 2001) cannot account for the intuition that some adverbs (e.g. *illegibly* in (74)) modify a manner (see Dik, 1975; Piñón, 2008; Schäfer, 2008). This intuition is corroborated by the observation that (74a) admits a paraphrase through a construction of the form *the way* ... (see (74b)).

(74)   a.   John wrote illegibly.
       ⇝ $(\exists e)[\mathbf{write}(e, \mathbf{john}) \wedge (\exists m)[\mathbf{manner}(m, e) \wedge \mathbf{illegible}(m)]]$
   ≡   b.   The way John wrote was illegible.

The Davidsonian treatment of manner adverbs as predicates of events further fails to account for the nonvalidity of inferences like (75) (Parsons, 1972, 131–133; see Schäfer, 2008). In the premise of this inference, i.e. (75a), *painstakingly* takes scope over *intelligible* (such that *painstakingly* does not specify the manner of John's writing, but the manner of his writing illegibly; Schäfer, 2006, 152). Since 'manner-free' semantics like Davidson's cannot capture such scope effects, they predict – falsely – that (75) is equivalent to (76a) and, hence, entails (76b). By allowing quantification over manners $m$ – and by adopting Eckardt's (1998) notion of a complex 'big event' $e^*$ – manner-based semantics block the inference in (75) as desired (Schäfer, 2008). In (75), $m$ is a variable over manners; '**part-of** $(e, e^*)$' expresses that the writing event $e$ is (spatio-temporally and informationally) included in the big event $e^*$.

(75)   a.   John painstakingly wrote illegibly.
            ['That John wrote illegibly was painstaking']
       ⇝ $(\exists e^*)[\mathbf{agent}(e, \mathbf{john}) \wedge (\exists e)[\mathbf{part\text{-}of}(e, e^*) \wedge \mathbf{write}(e, \mathbf{john}) \wedge$
       $(\exists m)[\mathbf{manner}(m, e) \wedge \mathbf{illegible}(m) \wedge \mathbf{painstaking}(e^*)]]]$
   ⇏   b.   ??John wrote painstakingly.

(76)   a.  ??John wrote painstakingly and illegibly.
       ⇝ $(\exists e)[\textbf{write}(e,\textbf{john}) \wedge \textbf{painstaking}(e) \wedge \textbf{illegible}(e)]$

$\stackrel{?}{\Rightarrow}$ b.  ??John wrote painstakingly.
       ⇝ $(\exists e)[\textbf{write}(e,\textbf{john}) \wedge \textbf{painstaking}(e)]$

Note that the existentially quantified manner $m$ in (75) is still dependent on some event $e$. This observation could lead one to the following conjecture about a universal semantic typology: The semantic ontology of any language will include manners only if it includes events. I will discuss conjectures of this form in Section 4.5.

### 4.2.2 Degrees

In contrast to the above, a commitment to degrees is supported by the observation that degree-free semantics (which try to model comparative constructions without reference to degrees; see Klein, 1980; McConnell-Ginet, 1973; Neeleman et al., 2004)[38] cannot easily account for explicit comparatives (Rett, 2022, 286–289). The latter are constructions like (77a) and (77b) that contain the comparative morpheme *-er* or the equative morpheme *as*.

(77)   a.  Jane is taller than Bill.
       b.  Jane is as tall as Susan.

Degree-based approaches (e.g. Cresswell, 1976; Heim, 2000; von Stechow, 1984) model comparative constructions by interpreting gradable predicates like *tall* as relations between individuals and degrees. They assume that formulas of the form '$\textbf{tall}(x,d)$' are true iff the measure of $x$ along the scale of height, $\mu_{\text{height}}(x)$, is at least $d$. Degree-based approaches treat comparative clauses as scope-taking expressions, where *-er* and *as* compare the maxima, $\textbf{max}(D)$ and $\textbf{max}(D')$, of two sets of degrees, $D$ and $D'$ (see Lassiter, 2012). The degree-based interpretation of (77a) is given in (78):

(78)   Jane is taller than Bill.
       ⇝ $\textbf{max}(\lambda d.\, \mu_{\text{height}}(\textbf{jane}) \geq d) > \textbf{max}(\lambda d.\, \mu_{\text{height}}(\textbf{bill}) \geq d)$

Since (78) involves lambda-abstraction over degrees (see the terms '$\lambda d.\, \mu_{\text{height}} (\ldots) \geq d$', which denote characteristic functions of sets of degrees), (78) prima facie provides an alternative to the Davidsonian/Quinean identification of ontological commitments from existential quantification. However, since degree-based approaches assume that degrees are downward monotone (such

---

[38] Instead of degrees, Klein (1980) uses equivalence classes of individuals (for (78): the class of equally tall individuals). For a discussion of the shortcomings of this approach, the reader is referred to Gehrke and Castroviejo (2015) and to Schäfer (2006).

that anyone who is $d$-tall is also $d'$-tall for all heights $d' < d$; Lassiter, 2012, 567) – and since '$\lambda d. \mu_{height}(\textbf{jane}) \geq d$' is a definite description of a degree (namely, the highest degree to which Jane is tall) –, the interpretation in (78) is even equivalent to the interpretation in (79).

(79)  $(\exists d)[(\mu_{height}(\textbf{jane}) \geq d) \wedge \neg(\mu_{height}(\textbf{bill}) \geq d)]$

Because (79) existentially quantifies over degrees, it again uses Quine's criterion of ontological commitment.

### 4.2.3 Times

Quine's strategy for the identification of ontological commitments further supports a category of times. This support is grounded in Comrie's definition of tense as "the grammaticalization of location in time" (Comrie, 1985, 1). It is reflected in the common assumption that tense morphemes (e.g. the English PAST morpheme -*ed*) contribute an existential quantifier over times (or time intervals; see the analysis of (80a–c)). In the interpretation in (80), $c$ is the actual utterance context; @ is the actual (evaluation) world. $t_c$ is the utterance time, $<$ is the relation of temporal precedence, and $\subseteq$ is the inclusion relation between time intervals.

(80)   a.   John calls Mary (in $c$ at @).
       ⇝  $(\exists t)[t_c \subseteq t \wedge \textbf{call}(@, t, \textbf{john}, \textbf{mary})]$
       b.   John called Mary (in $c$ at @).
       ⇝  $(\exists t)[t < t_c \wedge \textbf{call}(@, t, \textbf{john}, \textbf{mary})]$
       c.   John will call Mary (in $c$ at @).
       ⇝  $(\exists t)[t > t_c \wedge \textbf{call}(@, t, \textbf{john}, \textbf{mary})]$

The ability to linguistically access times or time intervals that are different from the utterance time (illustrated in (80b) and (80c)) is sometimes called *temporal displacement* (see Cariani, in press; Jaszczolt, 2020).

Interestingly, a commitment to times is even supported by superficially tenseless languages like St'át'imcets [Lillooet Salish] (Matthewson, 2006), Hausa (Mucha, 2013), Kalaallisut (Bittner, 2011), and Paraguayan Guaraní (Tonhauser, 2011). While these languages lack overt tense-marking (see the St'át'imcets sentence in (81)), their compositional semantics still manipulates times (Rett, 2022, 285). Such manipulation is required to explain why (81) can never receive a future-oriented interpretation, although it allows for a present and past-oriented interpretation (see the acceptability of (81a/b) and the deviance of (81c); Matthewson, 2006):

(81)  sáy'sez'-lhkan             (Matthewson, 2006, 676, ex. (4c))
      play-1SG.SUBJ
      'I played.' / 'I am playing.'

   a. sáy'sez'-lhkan  *lhkúnsa*     (see Matthewson, 2006, 677, ex. (5a))
      play-1SG.SUBJ *now*
      'I am playing now.'

   b. sáy'sez'-lhkan  *i-nátcw-as*  (see Matthewson, 2006, 677, ex. (5b))
      play-1SG.SUBJ *when.PAST-one.day.away-3CONJ*
      'I played yesterday.'

   c. *sáy'sez'-lhkan  *natcw/zánucwem*
                                     (Matthewson, 2006, 677, ex. (6c))
      play-1SG.SUBJ *one.day.away/next.year*
      'I will be playing tomorrow/next year.'

To capture the difference between (81a/b) and (81c), some researchers assume that superficially tenseless clauses like (81) contain a phonologically null tense morpheme, TENSE (see, e.g. Lee, 1999; Matthewson, 2006; Stowell, 1996). This morpheme picks out a reference time interval no part of which succeeds the utterance time (Matthewson, 2006, 680). Semantically, it contributes a context-dependent variable over time intervals that corresponds to the reference time (see (82a); cf. Partee, 1973, 1984). The resulting interpretation of the LF of (81) is given in (82b).[39] In this interpretation, $i$ is a variable over time intervals; $g$ is a contextually determined assignment function. $\tau(e)$ is the run time of the event $e$.

(82)  a. $[\![\text{TENSE}_i]\!]^{g,c}$ is only defined if $g(i) \leq t_c$
         If defined, $[\![\text{TENSE}_i]\!]^g = g(i)$

      b. $[\![\text{TENSE}_i\,[\text{PERF}\,[\text{sáy'sez'-lhkan}]]]\!]^{c,@}$
         $= (\exists e)[\textbf{play}(e, \textbf{speaker}(c)) \wedge \textbf{loc}(e) = @ \wedge \tau(e) \subseteq g(i)]$

The analysis in (82b) adopts an operator approach to tense. However, as Matthewson herself acknowledges (in Matthewson, 2006, 680), this choice is not key to her claim. An alternative to (82b) that involves overt existential quantification over times is given in (83):

(83)  $(\exists e)(\exists t)[\textbf{play}(e, \textbf{speaker}(c)) \wedge \textbf{loc}(e) = @ \wedge \textbf{time}(e) = t \wedge$
      $(t < t_c \vee t_c \subseteq t)]$

---

[39] For reasons of coherence (with reference to the example in (81) and the translations from Section 2.4.2), I deviate from Matthewson's semantics in some minor details.

This completes my review of familiar Quine-style arguments for the introduction of manners, degrees, and times. In the next subsection, I will present a series of arguments for the assumption of pluralities, vectors, and content individuals. Pluralities and content individuals differ from degrees, manners, and times since they are not (primarily) supported by Quine's quantificational criterion for ontological commitments. Rather, their introduction is motivated by the need to explain the distribution and selection behavior of certain kinds of expressions (e.g. the fact that *The boys gathered* – but not *Matti gathered* – is a semantically acceptable English sentence). I will describe such behavior in some detail in Section 4.3.1.

## 4.3 Coverage-Based Extensions II: Pluralities, Vectors, Content Individuals

### 4.3.1 Pluralities

To give a semantics for plurals (e.g. *horses*) and mass nouns (e.g. *water*) – and to capture the behavior of distributive and collective predicates (e.g. *gather*) – Link (1983) has proposed to extend Montague's domain of individuals, $A$, by pluralities. The latter are sums (or 'fusions') of individuals that are obtained from the elements of $A$ through a mereological sum operation, $\oplus$. The availability of such sums induces a partial ordering, $\leq$, (the parthood relation) on the extended individual domain (see also Landman, 1989a, 1989b). The possibility of sum formation already explains the cumulative reference property of plurals and mass terms (first noted by Quine, 1960; see the analysis in (84a) and (84b)). In (84b), **horses** abbreviates the result, $^{\circledast}$**horse**, of closing the set, $\{x : \mathbf{horse}(x)\}$, of individual horses under the mereological sum operation (see Link, 1983, 130). The example in (84a) originates from Link (1983, 128). The example in (84b) is due to Champollion and Brasoveanu (2022, 312).

(84)    a.    i.   $a$ is water and $b$ is water.    ⤳   $\mathbf{water}(a) \wedge \mathbf{water}(b)$
      ⇒    ii.   $a$ and $b$ taken together is water.   ⤳   $\mathbf{water}(a \oplus b)$

          b.    i.   The animals in this camp [= $c$] are horses and the animals in that camp [= $d$] are horses.    ⤳   $\mathbf{horses}(c) \wedge \mathbf{horses}(d)$
      ⇒    ii.   The animals in the two camps are horses.   ⤳   $\mathbf{horses}(c \oplus d)$

The difference between singular and plural count nouns accounts for the observation that plural noun phrases – like mass terms, but unlike singular count noun phrases – can occur without a determiner (such that they are 'bare'; see (85)) and are licensed by collective predicates like *gather* (see (86)):

(85)    I see water/horses/$^{??}$horse.

(86) a. The water gathered in big pools.
(Champollion & Brasoveanu, 2022, 312, (6b))

b. (The) Horses gathered around Mary.

c. *The/*A horse gathered around Mary.

According to Link, the domains of plurals and mass nouns differ with respect to the existence of minimal elements (or 'atoms') in the ordering ≤: Only the parthood relation for plurals – but not the relation for mass terms – has atomic elements. This difference explains the acceptability of (87b-ii) and the deviance of (87a-ii):

(87) a. i. much/little water

ii. *two/*many/*few water

b. i. *much/*little horses

ii. two/many/few horses

The above explanations are challenged by the observation that some count and mass nouns describe the same thing (e.g. *letters/mail, coins/change, leafs/foilage*; Chierchia, 1998, but see Grimm, 2012) and that some nouns (called 'hybrid nouns'; e.g. *chocolate, rope*) can be used as either count or mass nouns (see e.g. Gillon, 1999; Pelletier, 2012). These challenges notwithstanding, the addition of sums is generally taken to add to a semantics' adequacy.

### 4.3.2 Vectors

To give a compositional semantics for locative prepositional phrases (e.g. *behind the church, one meter behind the desk, far outside the village*), Zwarts (1997) and Zwarts and Winter (2000) have proposed to supplement the familiar stock of semantic categories with vectors (see also Winter, 2005). The latter are directed line segments that point from one location in space to another. On Zwarts' account, the prepositional phrase in these constructions is a set of vectors that represent positions (or regions) relative to the reference object. Specifically, this account interprets the region denoted by the PP *behind the church* as the set of vectors with their starting point at the church that point backwards. The theme of this PP is then located at the end point of one of these vectors. The truth-conditions of a sentence with this PP are given in (88) (Zwarts, 1997, 63–64), where $v$ is a variable over vectors:

(88) Jan is behind the church. (Zwarts, 1997, 63, ex. (18a))

⇝ $(\exists v)[\textbf{behind-the-church}(v) \land \textbf{loc}(\textbf{jan}, v)]$

The use of vectors is supported by their ability to explain the monotonicity of prepositions that admit locative modification (see Zwarts & Winter, 2000). The upward monotonicity of the preposition *in/inside* is exemplified in (89):

(89)    a.   The Babushka is in/inside the box.
         b.   The ball is in/inside the Babushka.
⇒   c.   The ball is in/inside the box.

Note that, its formal appeal notwithstanding, Zwarts and Winter's assumption of vectors is not (at all) widely shared in contemporary semantics. This even holds for competitor semantics for fragments with locative prepositional phrases and locative modifiers. These semantics interpret locative expressions through points (Wunderlich, 1991), sets of points (Kracht, 2002), or, respectively, through (individual) locations-as-individuals (Rothstein, 2020) (see (90)).

(90)    a.   {individuals, properties, ..., **vectors**}        (Zwarts & Winter)
         b.   {individuals, properties, ..., **points**}            (Wunderlich)
         c.   {individuals, properties, ..., **sets of points**}        (Kracht)
         d.   {individuals, properties, ..., **individual locations**}    (Rothstein)

Since Ritchie's (2016) Principle of Carrying Commitments (PCC) restricts a language's ontological commitments to those categories that are jointly (!) assumed by all competitor semantics (and hence, to a subset of the intersection of (90a) to (90d)), the ontology of a 'locative' fragment of English does not contain vectors.[40]

This contrasts with the result of applying PCC to semantics for fragments with content DPs (i.e. expressions like *the thought/rumor/claim that Fred left*; see Section 4.3.3). Since the vast majority of semantics for content DPs assumes abstract individuals with propositional content (so-called 'content individuals'), it could be argued that PCC supports a commitment to content individuals.

### 4.3.3 Content Individuals

Kratzer (2006) has proposed to extend Montague's individual domain $A$ by content individuals (see also Elliott, 2017; Moulton, 2009, 2015; as well as the

---

[40] I leave open the question (raised by Rothstein, 2020) of whether vectors, (sets of) points, and individual locations can be grouped together in an overarching category, namely, (sets of) spatial objects.

earlier, but differently targeted, Chierchia, 1984; Chierchia & Turner, 1988).[41] Content individuals are objects like thoughts, rumors, and claims (e.g. the claim that Fred left) that carry propositional information content (for the above: 'Fred left'). Kratzer assumes that the complements of attitude verbs and of verbs of saying denote properties of content individuals (for the above: the property of being an individual with the content 'Fred left'). The resulting semantics (in (91)) straightforwardly interprets reports with content DPs (e.g. (91b); see also Moulton, 2009), gives a uniform semantics for clausal arguments and direct objects (e.g. (91a)), and helps explain factivity inferences (e.g. the inference in (92); see Bondarenko, 2020). In (91), CONT is a function that maps an individual to its propositional content.[42]

(91)   a.   John claimed that Fred left.

⤳ $(\exists e)(\exists x)\big[\textbf{claim}(e, \textbf{john}, x) \wedge \text{CONT}(x) = \{w : \textbf{leave}(w, \textbf{fred})\}\big]$

    b.   Mary believes this claim, namely, that Fred left.

⤳ $(\exists e)\big[\textbf{believe}(e, \textbf{mary}, \iota x. \textbf{claim}(x) \wedge$
$\text{CONT}(x) = \{w : \textbf{leave}(w, \textbf{fred})\}\big)\big]$

(92)   a.   Kim knows that it is raining in Bochum.
  ⇒ b.   It is raining in Bochum.

All of my previous arguments have motivated different extensions of Montague's ontology. Only a very small line of work has argued for the converse: the reduction of this ontology (in the case of Keenan (2018): dropping individuals). For completeness – and since Keenan's ontology will play a central role in my discussion of intertheoretic and inter-ontology relations in Section 5 – I sketch this work in the next subsection.

### 4.4 'Pruning' the Ontology: Drop Individuals

Bucking the trend to model new or challenging phenomena through the addition of further entities (or semantic categories), Keenan (2015, 2018) has proposed to drop Montague's individual domain $A$ in favor of a Boolean-structured set of primitive [= unanalyzable, non-decomposable] properties (see

---

[41] Similar ideas have been put forth by Moltmann (2013b, 2017, 2020b), who calls such entities 'content-bearing objects'. Chierchia and Turner's Property Theory (1988) assumes type-$e$ correlates of all propositions, which their theory calls 'information units' and treats as urelements. Information units differ from Kratzer-style content individuals in standing in a one-to-one relation to propositions. As a result of this relation, different information units cannot be correlates of the same proposition, unlike different content individuals (which may share the same propositional content).

[42] Most works in the Kratzerian tradition assume that CONT takes two arguments, namely, a content individual $x$ and a world $w$, and returns the propositional content of $x$ at $w$ (see e.g. Moulton, 2015, 312). I here suppress the world argument for simplicity.

also Keenan & Faltz, 1985). The latter are hyperfine-grained entities whose identity-conditions are not given by extensional or intensional equivalence. As a result, two primitive properties (e.g. 'be a groundhog' and 'be a woodchuck') may be distinct even if they are exemplified by exactly the same individuals in all possible worlds. The hyperfine individuation of properties facilitates a more adequate modelling of attitude contexts that does not predict a version of logical omniscience (see (93)).[43] This version falsely predicts the agent's (here: Bill's) relation to all co-extensional and co-intensional properties (incl. 'be a woodchuck') from the agent's relation to a single property (here: 'be a groundhog').

(93) a. Bill is imagining a groundhog. ⇝ **imagine(bill, groundhog)**

b. All groundhogs are woodchucks, and *vice versa*.

⇝ $(\forall w)(\forall x)[\textbf{groundhog}_w(x) \leftrightarrow \textbf{woodchuck}_w(x)]$

⇎ c. Bill is imagining a woodchuck. ⇝ **imagine(bill, woodchuck)**

Since Keenan's semantics replaces Montagovian sets of individuals (or functions from individuals to propositions) by primitive properties, it straightforwardly captures the non-extensionality of evaluative adjectives like *skillful* (interpreted as restricting functions from properties to properties). This non-extensionality is evidenced by the invalidity of extensionality-based inferences like (94),[44] where $\mathfrak{F}$ is a variable over properties of properties (see Keenan, 2015, 396–397):

(94) a. John is a skillful surgeon. ⇝ **john(skillful(surgeon))**

b. All surgeons are flautists, and *vice versa*.

⇝ $(\forall \mathfrak{F})[\mathfrak{F}(\textbf{surgeon}) \leftrightarrow \mathfrak{F}(\textbf{flautist})]$

⇎ c. John is a skillful flautist. ⇝ **john(skillful(flautist))**

Note that, while Keenan's semantics models (94) without recourse to individuals, it is doubtful whether this semantics can rid itself of individuals altogether. Rather, it seems that this semantics still assumes individuals in the metatheory. This is suggested by Keenan's description of (the content of) a primitive property $\mathfrak{P}$ as "what we have to know [in order] to know whether an arbitrary individual has [$\mathfrak{P}$]" (Keenan, 2015, 386).

---

[43] This version differs from standard versions of logical omniscience (see Hintikka, 1975) in (i) involving properties (rather than propositions) and in (ii) predicting the agent's relation to all co-intensional properties (rather than to all necessarily true propositions).

[44] To compensate for the absence of individual referents of proper names, Keenan interprets *John* in (94) as a set of primitive properties. As a result, *John is a surgeon* is interpreted as ⟦John⟧ (⟦surgeon⟧) (analogously to its interpretation on Montague's strategy of 'generalizing to the worst case').

## 4.5 Local versus Global Ontology: Ontologies of Other Languages

My discussion from Section 4.2 has already suggested that – like differently rich fragments of the same language – different languages may presuppose different semantic ontologies. Section 4.2.3 has questioned such a difference for a commitment to times (or time intervals). The above notwithstanding, work on comparatives has suggested that some languages do not assume a semantic category of degrees. These languages include Motu (see Beck et al., 2009), Washo (see Bochnak, 2015), Walpiri (see Bowler, 2016), and Nez Perce (see Deal & Hohaus, 2019). In particular, Beck et al. (2009) have shown that Motu, an Austronesian language of Papua New Guinea, lacks a dedicated degree morphology, and allows neither difference comparatives nor comparison with a degree. To compensate for the non-availability of comparative morphology, Motu speakers use a conjunctive strategy (exemplified in (95)) that juxtaposes two full clauses containing antonymous predicates.

(95)   Mary na lata, to Frank na kwadōgi.         (Beck et al., 2009, 3)
       Mary TOP tall, but Frank TOP short.
       'Mary is tall, but Frank is short.'   (≡ 'Mary is taller than Frank.')

Beck et al.'s semantics for (95) (in (96); see also Bochnak, 2015) contains neither a measure function nor a degree variable. Instead, it interprets gradable predicates like *tall* as context-sensitive vague predicates (namely, 'counts as tall in $c$'; see Bochnak, 2015):

(96)   $[\![(95)]\!]^c = \textbf{tall}(c, \textbf{mary}) \wedge \textbf{short}(c, \textbf{frank})$

The absence of reference to – or quantification over – degrees in this semantics suggests that the semantic ontology of Motu (like the ontology of Montague's PTQ-fragment) does not contain degrees.

Interestingly, degree-freeness may even hold of the ontologies of languages with gradable adjectives and a dedicated comparative morpheme, like Nez Perce (see Deal & Hohaus, 2019): Deal and Hohaus have shown that, while Nez Perce has a Klein-style comparative operator (see Klein, 1980), it witnesses a negative setting, [−DSP], of the Degree Semantics Parameter (see Beck et al., 2009). In virtue of its Klein-style comparative operator, Nez Perce allows the manipulation of context. Because of its negative DSP-setting, Nez Perce does not have predicates that introduce degree arguments.

It remains an open question whether language-specific ontological differences like the one above also hold for other semantic categories. This applies, for example, to Bogal-Allbritten and Coppock's (2020) claim (reported in Rett,

2022, 288, fn. 5) that Navajo has degrees and degree quantifiers, but lacks individual quantifiers. A similar question would be whether the semantic ontologies of all languages include manners. In particular, it stands to reason that, if a given language were to lack all expressions (e.g. adverbs like *illegibly*; see Section 4.2.1) whose semantic analysis has been taken to involve manners, it would not be committed to manners.

Independently of the answers to the above questions, the difference in commitment to degrees between English and Motu already suggests that the semantic ontology varies (to some extent) from language to language. While the precise extent of such cross-linguistic ontological variation is a matter of future investigation, I assume with Grimm and McNally (2022) that "[i]f it can be shown that a particular ontological type can be identified in language after language ... this greatly supports including that type in our natural language ontology" (p. 273).

To acknowledge the existence of cross-linguistic ontological differences, I will hereafter refer to the shared ontological commitments of all languages as the *global (semantic) ontology* of natural language. I will call the specific ontological commitments of individual languages or fragments the *local (semantic) ontology* of the relevant language/fragment, and call a theory's specific ontological commitments – which may contain many more semantic categories than the (cross-theoretically robust) local ontology[45] – the *special (semantic) ontology*. I expect that the global ontology will include individuals, propositions, properties, and – on some accounts – possible worlds and times (among others). Local ontologies will differ at least with respect to their inclusion of degrees (see the beginning of this subsection). Special ontologies will diverge with regard to their inclusion of, for example, individuals (see Section 4.4), manners (see Section 4.2.1), and vectors (see Section 4.3.2).

This completes my survey of the descriptive semantic ontology of (fragments of) natural language(s). The next section investigates the relations between different special and local ontologies, and identifies the merits of relating different such ontologies and their semantic categories.

## 5 Relating Different Ontologies

My comparison of different local ontologies (in Section 4.5) has already shown that the ontologies of (reasonably rich fragments of) some languages are included in the ontologies of other languages. Thus, while the ontologies of

---

[45] This is a consequence of Ritchie's (2016) Principle of Carrying Commitments, which restricts a language's ontological commitments to those categories that are jointly assumed by all competitor semantic theories (see Section 1.2).

English and Motu share a commitment to individuals, properties, and propositions (among others), only the ontology of English has a commitment to degrees (such that the semantic ontology of Motu is properly included in the ontology of English; see (97)).

(97) a.  Motu: {individuals, properties, ..., propositions}
⊆ b.  English: {individuals, properties, ..., propositions, **degrees**}

In virtue of this inclusion, any word or phrase of Motu (expectedly) has an interpretation in the semantic ontology of English, but not the other way around (at least not for degree modifiers and explicit comparatives).

Below, I will first show that the phenomenon of ontology inclusion is also attested at the level of special ontologies. I will then describe the merits of 'translating' semantic theories (with a given special ontology) into the ontology of a different semantic theory (both in Section 5.1). The section closes by showing the merits of identifying inter-category relations within the ontology of a single semantic theory (in Section 5.2).

## 5.1 Inter-theory Relations

My discussion of Ritchie's (2016) Principle of Carrying Commitments has already suggested that a similar situation to the one in (97) holds for a single language's special ontologies. Since they involve different extensions of the local ontology (through different semantic categories), some of these ontologies can properly contain the ontologies of other theories (for the same fragment). This holds, for example, for the ontologies from Montague (1973) and Keenan (2015, 2018): Since Keenan's ontology lacks a category of individuals (at least at the object level; see Section 4.4), it is properly included in Montague's ontology from Section 3. The resulting relation between these two ontologies is captured in (98):

(98) a.  Keenan: {properties, GQs, ..., propositions}
⊆ b.  Montague: {properties, GQs, ..., propositions, **individuals**}

Similar inclusion relations obtain between the ontologies from (6) in Section 1.2 (copied, with added inclusion relations, in (99)):

(99) a.  {properties}
⊆ b.  {individuals, properties}
   c.  {properties, generalized quantifiers}
⊆ d.  {individuals, properties, generalized quantifiers}

Since Montague's and Keenan's ontologies target overlapping fragments, I assume – for ease of exposition – that the semantic categories that are shared by these ontologies (e.g. property, generalized quantifier) contain exactly the same elements. Thus, if Keenan's ontology contains the property **flautist**, so will (or should) Montague's ontology. That the latter is not the case (see the list of Montague's property-denoting expressions in Table 2) already shows that inter-ontology relations are more complex than the above idealized presentation suggests.

To provide a better – more realistic – assessment of inter-ontology relations like the above, one would first need to extend the PTQ-fragment via the expressions from Keenan's fragment (incl. the nouns *flautist* and *surgeon* as well as the adjective *skillful*), and enrich the relevant domains in Montagovian models with Keenan's semantic values of these expressions (or of their logical translations, **flautist**, **surgeon**, and **skillful**; see (94)).

Since Keenan's ontology analogously lacks some expressions from the PTQ-fragment (e.g. *fish*, *temperature*, *rise*), it requires a similar move. However, because of Keenan's renunciation of individuals, this move cannot simply lie in 'importing' the relevant (terms and) objects from Montague's models. Rather, these objects must be 'lifted' (e.g. by a function ↑) to their representations in a category from Keenan's ontology.[46] For individuals (e.g. $x$ [↞ $he_0$]) and relations between individuals (e.g. **find**), these representations can be generalized quantifiers (here: $\mathfrak{Q}$ [:= ↑$x$]) and, respectively, relations between pairs of generalized quantifiers (here: 𝔣𝔦𝔫𝔡 [:= ↑**find**]).

The resulting semantics for sentences like (67b) (whose original Montagovian version is copied in (100a)) is given in (100b). For simplicity, the interpretations in (100) ignore world arguments. In (100b), 𝔱𝔯𝔶-𝔱𝔬 is a relation between a generalized quantifier (e.g. the quantifier denoted by '**john**') and a property of generalized quantifiers (e.g. the property $\lambda\mathfrak{Q}\exists\mathfrak{O}. \mathfrak{O}(\textbf{unicorn}) \wedge \mathfrak{find}(\mathfrak{Q},\mathfrak{O})$). $\mathfrak{Q}$ and $\mathfrak{O}$ are variables over generalized quantifiers.

(100)  John tries [that [$\lambda y_1$. PRO$_1$ finds a unicorn]]

⤳ a. **try-to**(**john**, $\lambda y \exists x.$ **unicorn**$(x) \wedge$ **find**$(y,x)$)

⤳ b. 𝔱𝔯𝔶-𝔱𝔬(**john**, $\lambda\mathfrak{Q}\exists\mathfrak{O}. \mathfrak{O}($**unicorn**$) \wedge \mathfrak{find}(\mathfrak{Q},\mathfrak{O}))$
[alternatively: 𝔱𝔯𝔶-𝔱𝔬(**john**, $\lambda\mathfrak{Q}. \mathfrak{find}'(\mathfrak{Q},$ **unicorn**$))$]

---

[46] Since Keenan's ontology contains more-finely-grained objects than Montague's ontology (Keenan's primitive properties are not individuated by their extensions across possible worlds), this lifting must also involve a hyperintensional representation of intensions. An example of such representation is the coding of propositional functions as primitive properties. To reduce complexity, I here ignore this issue. This is reflected in my use of the same non-logical constants for Montague's intensional and for Keenan's hyperintensional properties.

The possibility of extending semantic theories via objects – or even via semantic categories – from other theories has a substantial merit: It allows us to unify the results from different theories. Thus, by extending Montague's ontology from Section 3 via primitive properties (incl. zero-place properties, i.e. primitive propositions), we obtain a larger-scope version of Montague semantics. This version provides an adequate interpretation of evaluate adjectives like *skillful* that blocks counterintuive inferences like (94). Since primitive properties can distinguish between propositions that are true in exactly the same possible worlds (or situations), the resulting semantics further explains the non-validity of inferences like (101) (based on Pollard, 2008), contra what would be predicted by a 'classical' Montague-style semantics.

(101)    a.   Bill believes that Punxsutawney Phil is a groundhog.
           b.   In all possible worlds/situations, all groundhogs are woodchucks.
   ⇏   c.   Bill believes that Punxsutawney Phil is a woodchuck.

For a detailed description of such extensions and inter-model 'translations,' the interested reader is referred to Liefke (2018) (see also Muskens, 2005; Thomason, 1980).

Inversely to what is described above, the ontologies of specific semantic theories (for a given linguistic fragment) can also be reduced to 'poorer' ontologies (with fewer categories) that, however, still model the original fragment. Such reduction is achieved by eliminating worlds and/or individual concepts from a possible worlds-version of Keenan's hyperintensional semantics, and by eliminating manners from a compositional version of event semantics. In particular, since possible worlds can be analyzed as special sets of propositions (namely, as ultrafilters on propositions; see Fox et al., 2002; Pollard, 2008), the ontology of a modal hyperintensional semantics does not require primitive possible worlds next to primitive propositions. The same holds for propositions and individual concepts (since individual concepts can be analyzed as propositional functions, see Kaplan's (1976) coding strategy, sketched in Section 3.2) and for events and manners (since manners can be analyzed as similarity classes of events; see Umbach et al., 2022).

Inter-ontology reductions like the above have a number of significant merits: Firstly, they allow us to transfer the interpretive success (*re* explanatory and predictive power) of one theory (with particular ontological commitments) to another theory (with different ontological commitments). For example, such transfer finds that, if a semantics with a possible worlds-ontology can provide an adequate interpretation of modals (see Section 2.4.3), then so can its 'world-free' version – at least so long as it assumes primitive propositions.

In virtue of this transfer, inter-ontology reductions will further yield insight into the requirements on ontologically 'minimal' semantic theories for certain linguistic phenomena, and will contribute to a better understanding of natural language's semantic ontology (see Liefke, 2014, 2018). I will provide an in-depth discussion of such reduction relations in the sequel to this Element, which frames this discussion against the background of simple type theory.

## 5.2 Inter-category Relations

My observations about the reducibility/analyzability of possible worlds and manners already suggest that relations between different semantic categories can also hold <u>within</u> the ontology of a single semantic theory. At a pre-theoretical level, these relations are captured by our prose descriptions of actual and possible states of affairs. Thus, we talk of individuals *having* ('exemplifying' or 'instantiating') properties and *performing* ('partaking' or 'engaging in') activities, of propositions *being true at* (or 'holding in') possible worlds, of events *showing* (or 'illustrating') manners, and of propositions *answering* (or 'deciding') questions.

At the more formal level of compositional semantics, these diverse relations are uniformly captured in terms of semantic composition (commonly analyzed through Functional Application; see Section 1). In the examples below, **matti** is an individual constant, while Q stands proxy for a polar question (e.g. 'Was John singing?').

(102)   a.  Matti [$_{VP}$is a boy].          ⤳ **boy**(**matti**)       (having a property)
       b.  Matti [$_{VP}$is sleeping]. ⤳ **sleep**(**matti**)   (performing an activity)
       c.  It [$_{VP}$is raining].           ⤳ **rain**(@)              (being true [at a world])
       d.  It$_1$ [= J's writing] is slow. ⤳ **slow**($e_1$)        (showing a manner)
       e.  Q? – yes (namely, *p*)!        ⤳ **Q**(*p*)                (answering a question)

The above suggests that the semantic categories within a single ontology are pervasively related. This was already asserted in the introduction to this Element, where I stated that "compositional semantics requires ... (iii) an account of the interaction of meanings from different classes" (Section 1). The existence of cross-categorial relations is reinforced by the observation that complex semantic values arise from the compositional interaction of different, related objects. Thus, to yield a lower-type interpretation of (94a) (that interprets *John* as an individual, i.e. **john**; in (103)), it does not suffice to relate individuals (here: **john**) to properties (here: **surgeon** [≡ $\lambda x.$ **surgeon**(*x*)]) and, respectively, to relate properties to property-to-property functions (here:

# Natural Language Ontology and Semantic Theory

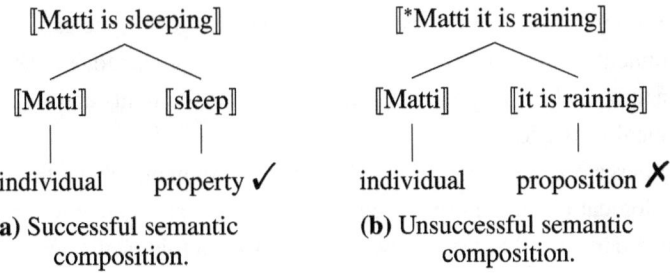

**Figure 3** A successful and an unsuccessful case of semantic composition.

**skillful**). Rather, individuals must also be related to property-to-property functions. This relation is captured in the compositional contribution of *skillful* in (103a) (note the processing of the individual variable $x$):

(103) ⟦John [<sub>VP</sub>is a skillful surgeon]⟧ = (⟦skillful⟧(⟦surgeon⟧))(⟦John⟧)

= a. $(\lambda P \lambda x.(\textbf{skillful}(P))(x))(⟦\text{surgeon}⟧)(⟦\text{John}⟧)$

≡ b. $(\lambda x.(\textbf{skillful}(\textbf{surgeon}))(x))(⟦\text{John}⟧)$

≡ c. $(\textbf{skillful}(\textbf{surgeon}))(\textbf{john})$

Since this Element is dedicated to descriptive natural language ontology, I confine my elaborations of inter-category relations to the above example. A comprehensive discussion of such relations will be provided in the sequel Element, entitled *Reduction and Unification in Natural Language Ontology*. To prepare this discussion – and since the following considerations are independently interesting – I close this Element by giving reasons for identifying cross-categorial relations:

My example in (103) has already shown that inter-category relations are the driving force behind compositionality. These relations moreover provide an internal type checking mechanism. This mechanism is enabled by the treatment of semantic composition as (forward or backward) Functional Application (see (2) in Section 1), and by the assumption that functions only accept arguments of a certain type/semantic category, namely, of those categories to which they are intuitively related (see Section 2.2). The observation that individuals in an intuitive sense 'have' properties, but not propositions (see (102)) thus explains the acceptability of (1a)/(104a) (see Fig. 3a) and the deviance of (104b) (see Fig. 3b).

(104)  a. Matti is sleeping.
       b. *Matti it is raining.

As is suggested by Umbach et al.'s analysis of manners as similarity classes of events, inter-category relations further help tame Bach's (1986b) ontological 'zoo': By constructing the elements in some of the semantic categories from Sections 3–4 from the elements of other categories, we can reduce our commitment to a small(er) set of primitive semantic categories. This reduction, in turn, enables the previous account of compositionality and helps explain selectional restrictions.

The described reduction of ontological commitments obeys the principle of ontological parsimony (more commonly known as *Ockham's razor*). This principle demands that the number of entities or ontological categories that a specific theory assumes should not be increased beyond necessity (Clauberg, 2009, 320). When applied to the ontology of natural language semantics, Ockham's principle demands that ontological categories should only be adopted if the semantic phenomena that they are intended to explain resist an explanation through those categories that are assumed anyway.

Importantly, the Ockhamian promotion of categorial parsimony comes at a price, namely, an (at least partial) loss of simplicity: While the objects of 'reduced' categories were simple *pre*-reduction (in the sense that they did not have internal structure), they are complex *post*-reduction (when they take the form of sets, similarity classes, or functions). The trade-off between simplicity and parsimony in natural language ontology is an emergent topic in semantics and the philosophy of language that has only recently started to gain attention (see e.g. Liefke, 2021; Liefke & Werning, 2018; Sutton, 2024; Theiler et al., 2018).

## 6 Conclusion: Finding the Perfect Ontology?

My discussion in this Element has shown that the construction of a semantic ontology (for a single language, or for all documented natural languages) is a challenging task. This holds especially in light of the plethora of linguistic phenomena, the different size of linguistic fragments, and the diversity of methodological goals. This Element has suggested that the different strategies for identifying a language's semantic commitment may arrive at (partly) different ontologies. This holds, for example, for the lexical and the logical-semantic strategy, of which only the latter attests the PTQ-fragment a commitment to individuals. In this regard, the results of applying competing 'commitment-identifying' strategies align remarkably well with the ontological commitments of different semantic theories (see, for example, Montague, 1973 vs. Keenan, 2015).

My review of the ontology-conscious semantic literature (in Sections 3–4) has found that – the above notwithstanding – the descriptive ontologies of different natural languages converge to a surprising extent (see esp. Section 4.5). This holds at least for individuals, propositions, properties, and (possibly) times – even if not for degrees, and perhaps also not for manners.

The close relation between different ontologies becomes significantly looser when one moves from the question of which ontological categories are used in day-to-day semantic theorizing to the question of which ontological categories are minimally required to interpret a given language or fragment: Depending on whether semantic work focuses on compositionality (and associated semantic explanations of grammaticality) or on cognitive plausibility (and associated issues of hyperintensionality), it will endorse or oppose its ontology's reduction to a small set of ontological primitives. A similar observation holds for work that is primarily interested in describing/explaining semantic phenomena and for work that is more interested in foundational questions.

The Element has shown that, even in different contexts of knowledge acquisition like foundational vis-à-vis applied projects, there are hard conditions on semantic ontology engineering:

① On the one hand, ontologies must contain as many semantic categories as are required (by at least one of the strategies from Section 2) to interpret the target linguistic fragment.

② On the other hand, according to Ockham's razor, ontologies may not assume categories that are not necessary for this interpretation, by any of the familiar strategies.

The above requirements identify a lower bound (①) and an upper bound (②) for the number of semantic categories.

The precise effect of these requirements varies with the respective semantic endeavor: Because of their greater interest in empirical scope and accuracy, applied projects will likely 'need' a larger number of semantic categories (by the above conditions) than foundational projects. This also holds since applied projects are often not aware of – or not interested in – the possibility of reducing categories. After all, working with a larger set of categories facilitates day-to-day semantics. Because of their greater interest in parsimony and inter-category relations, foundational projects will require noticeably fewer categories than applied projects. As a result, foundational ontologies will better suit Quine's (1948) "taste for desert landscapes."

Contemporary semantics and the philosophy of language witness examples of both extremes on the 'zoo'/'desert'-spectrum. Far on the 'zoo' side (with a plethora of ontological categories) stand semantics for nominalized constructions (that distinguish between facts, states of affairs, events, and event types; see e.g. Grimm & McNally, 2015, 2022; Zucchi, 2013), Kratzer-style semantics for clausal complements (that assume different categories of propositional, attitudinal, and modal objects; see e.g. Kratzer, 2006; Moltmann, 2013b), and theories of dialogue modelling (like Ginzburg's (2012) KoS, which uses a rich type theory with distinct categories for events, states, and various abstract entities).

Far on the 'desert' side (with few categories) stand theories like inquisitive semantics (InqS; see Ciardelli et al., 2018) and my single-type semantics (STS; see Liefke, 2021; Liefke & Werning, 2018). Both of these theories seek to merge intuitively distinct semantic categories (in InqS: propositions and questions; in STS: propositions and individuals) into a single, unified, category (namely, questions in InqS; situated propositions [or parametrized centered questions] in STS).

Much of the literature that was cited in this Element lies in the middle range of the 'zoo'/'desert'-spectrum. It will be the privilege of future research to see how these trends develop and whether this development will bring about changes in the ontologies surveyed here.

# References

Ajdukiewicz, K. (1935). Die syntaktische Konnexität. *Studia Philosophica*, *1*, 1–27.

Alexeyenko, S. (2015). The Syntax and Semantics of Manner Modification: Adjectives and adverbs (Unpublished doctoral dissertation). University of Osnabrück.

Anderson, C., & Morzycki, M. (2015). Degrees as kinds. *Natural Language and Linguistic Theory*, *33*(3), 791–828.

Asher, N. (1993). *Reference to Abstract Objects in Discourse* (Vol. 50). Kluwer Academic Publishers.

Bach, E. (1986a). The algebra of events. *Linguistics and Philosophy*, *9*(1), 5–16.

Bach, E. (1986b). Natural language metaphysics. In R.B. Marcus, G.J.W. Dorn, & P. Weingartner (Eds.), *Logic, Methodology and Philosophy of Science VII* (pp. 573–593). Elsevier.

Bar-Hillel, Y. (1953). A quasi-arithmetical notation for syntactic description. *Language*, *29*(1), 47–58.

Barwise, J., & Perry, J. (1983). *Situations and Attitudes*. MIT Press.

Beck, S., Krasikova, S., Fleischer, D., Gergel, R., Hofstetter, S., Savelsberg, C., Vanderelst, J., & Villalta, E. (2009). Crosslinguistic variation in comparison constructions. *Linguistic Variation Yearbook*, *9*, 1–66.

Betti, A. (2015). *Against Facts*. MIT Press.

Bittner, M. (2001). Topical referents for individuals and possibilities. *Semantics and Linguistic Theory (SALT)*, *11*, 36–55.

Bittner, M. (2011). Time and modality without tenses or modals. In R. Musan & M. Rathers (Eds.), *Tense Across Languages* (pp. 147–188). De Gruyter.

Blumberg, K. (2019). Desire, Imagination, and the Many-Layered Mind (Unpublished doctoral dissertation). New York University.

Bochnak, R. (2015). The degree semantics parameter and cross-linguistic variation. *Semantics and Pragmatics*, *8*(6), 1–48.

Bondarenko, T. (2020). Factivity from pre-existence. *Glossa*, *5*(1), 109.

Bowler, M. (2016). The status of degrees in Walpiri. In M. Grubic & A. Mucha (Eds.), *Proceedings of the Semantics of African, Asian and Austronesian Languages 2* (pp. 1–17). University of Potsdam.

Cariani, F. (in press). Future displacement and modality. In E. Lepore & U. Stojnic (Eds.), *Oxford Handbook of Philosophy of Language*, 2nd edition. Oxford University Press. https://philpapers.org/go.pl?id=CARFDA-4&proxyId=&u=https%3A%2F%2Fphilpapers.org%2Farchive%2FCARFDA-4.pdf.

Carlson, G.N. (1977). Reference to Kinds in English (Unpublished doctoral dissertation). University of Massachusetts, Amherst.

Champollion, L., & Brasoveanu, A. (2022). On Link's "The logical analysis of plurals and mass terms: A lattice-theoretical approach". In L. McNally & Z.G. Szabó (Eds.), *A Reader's Guide to Classic Papers in Formal Semantics* (pp. 331–366). Springer.

Charlow, S. (2014). On the Semantics of Exceptional Scope (Unpublished doctoral dissertation). New York University.

Chierchia, G. (1984). Topics in the Syntax and Semantics of Infinitives and Gerunds (Unpublished doctoral dissertation). University of Massachusetts, Amherst.

Chierchia, G. (1998). Plurality of mass nouns and the notion of 'semantic parameter'. In S. Rothstein (Ed.), *Events and Grammar* (pp. 53–103). Springer.

Chierchia, G., & Turner, R. (1988). Semantics and property theory. *Linguistics and Philosophy*, *11*(3), 261–302.

Ciardelli, I., Groenendijk, J., & Roelofsen, F. (2018). *Inquisitive Semantics*. Oxford University Press.

Ciardelli, I., Roelofsen, F., & Theiler, N. (2017). Composing alternatives. *Linguistics and Philosophy*, *40*(1), 1–36.

Clauberg, J. (2009). *Logica vetus et nova (1658)*. Kessinger Publishing.

Colapinto, A. (2020). *Do it* anaphora without covert events: In defense of a pro-verb analysis. *Lingua*, *245*, 102921.

Comrie, B. (1985). *Tense*. Cambridge Textbooks in Linguistics (Vol. 17). Cambridge University Press.

Contini-Morava, E. (2000). Noun class as number in Swahili. In *Amsterdam Studies in the Theory and History of the Linguistic Science* (Vol. 4, pp. 3–30). John Benjamins.

Cooper, R. (2023). *From Perception to Communication: A theory of types for action and meaning* (Vol. 16). Oxford University Press.

Cresswell, M.J. (1973). *Logics and Languages*. Methuen.

Cresswell, M.J. (1976). The semantics of degree. In B. Partee (Ed.), *Montague Grammar* (pp. 261–292). Elsevier.

Cresswell, M.J. (1990). *Entities and Indices*. Springer.

Crouch, D., & King, T.H. (2008). Type-checking in formally non-typed systems. In *Software Engineering, Testing, and Quality Assurance for Natural Language Processing* (pp. 3–4). Association for Computational Linguistics.

Curry, H.B. (1961). Some logical aspects of grammatical structure. In R. Jakobson (Ed.), *Structure of Language and its Mathematical Aspects* (Vol. 12, pp. 56–68). American Mathematical Society.

D'Ambrosio, J. (2023). Prior's puzzle generalized. *Philosophy and Phenomenological Research, 106*(1), 196–220.

D'Ambrosio, J., & Stoljar, D. (2021). Vendler's puzzle about imagination. *Synthese, 199*, 12923–12944.

Davidson, D. (1967). Truth and meaning. *Synthese, 17*(3), 304–323.

Davidson, D. (1977). The method of truth in metaphysics. *Midwest Studies in Philosophy, 2*(1), 244–254.

Davidson, D. (2001). The logical form of action sentences. In D. Davidson (Ed.), *Essays on Actions and Events: Philosophical essays of Donald Davidson* (pp. 105–121). Clarendon Press.

Deal, A. R., & Hohaus, V. (2019). Vague predicates, crisp judgments. In M.T. Espinal, E. Castroviejo, M. Leonetti, L. McNally, & C. Real-Puigdollers (Eds.), *Proceedings of Sinn und Bedeutung 23* (Vol. 1, pp. 347–364). Autonomous University of Barcelona.

Degtyarenko, K., de Matos, P., Ennis, M., Hastings, J., Zbinden, M., McNaught, R., A. Alcántara, Darsow, M., Guedj, M., & Ashburner, M. (2008, 01). Chebi: A database and ontology for chemical entities of biological interest. *Nucleic Acids Research, 36*, D344–350.

Dik, S.C. (1975). The semantic representation of manner adverbials. In A. Kraak (Ed.), *Linguistics in the Netherlands 1972–1973* (pp. 96–121). Van Gorcum.

Dowty, D. (1991). Thematic proto-roles and argument selection. *Language, 67*(3), 547–619.

Eckardt, R. (1998). *Adverbs, Events, and Other Things*. Niemeyer.

Elliott, P. (2017). Elements of Clausal Embedding (Unpublished doctoral dissertation). University College London.

Engesser, K. (1980). *Untersuchungen zur Montaguegrammatik* (Unpublished doctoral dissertation). University of Konstanz.

Fara, D.G. (2015). Names are predicates. *Philosophical Review, 124*(1), 59–117.

Fernando, T. (1993). The donkey strikes back: Extending the dynamic interpretation 'constructively'. In *Sixth Conference of the European Chapter of the Association for Computational Linguistics* (pp. 130–138). Publisher: OTS-Research Institute for Language and Speech, Utrecht University.

Fillmore, C.J. (1982). Frame semantics. In *Linguistics in the Morning Calm* (pp. 111–137). Hanshin.

Fine, K. (2003). The non-identity of a material thing and its matter. *Mind*, *112*(446), 195–234.

Fine, K. (2017). Naïve metaphysics. *Philosophical Issues*, *27*(1), 98–113.

Forbes, G. (2006). *Attitude Problems: An essay on linguistic intensionality*. Oxford University Press.

Forbes, G. (2018). Content and theme in attitude ascriptions. In A. Grzankowski & M. Montague (Eds.), *Non-Propositional Intentionality* (pp. 114–133). Oxford University Press.

Fox, C., Lappin, S., & Pollard, C. (2002). A higher-order fine-grained logic for intensional semantics. In G. Alberti, K. Balough, & P. Dekker (Eds.), *Proceedings of the Seventh Symposium for Logic and Language* (pp. 37–46). Pécs University.

Frege, G. (1997). Über Sinn und Bedeutung [on *Sinn* and *Bedeutung*]. In M. Beaney (Ed.), *The Frege Reader* (pp. 151–171). Blackwell.

Gallin, D. (1975). *Intensional and Higher-Order Modal Logic*. North-Holland.

Gamut, L. (1991). *Logic, Language, and Meaning, Volume 2: Intensional logic and logical grammar*. University of Chicago Press.

Gehrke, B., & Castroviejo, E. (2015). Manner and degree: An introduction. *Natural Language and Linguistic Theory*, *33*, 745–790.

Gillon, B. (1999). The lexical semantics of English count and mass nouns. In E. Viegas (Ed.), *The Breadth and Depth of Semantic Lexicons* (pp. 19–37). Kluwer.

Ginzburg, J. (1995). Resolving questions, II. *Linguistics and Philosophy*, *18*(5), 567–609.

Ginzburg, J. (2005). Situation semantics: The ontological balance sheet. *Research on Language and Computation*, *3*(2), 363–389.

Ginzburg, J. (2008). Situation semantics and the ontology of natural language. In C. Maienborn, K. von Heusinger, & P. Portner (Eds.), *Semantics: Theories* (pp. 267–294). Mouton de Gruyter.

Ginzburg, J. (2012). *The Interactive Stance: Meaning for conversation*. Oxford University Press.

Grimm, S. (2012). Number and Individuation (Unpublished doctoral dissertation). Stanford University.

Grimm, S., & McNally, L. (2015). The *-ing* dynasty. *Semantics and Linguistic Theory (SALT)*, *25*, 82–102.

Grimm, S., & McNally, L. (2022). Nominalization and natural language ontology. *Annual Review of Linguistics*, *8*(1), 257–277.

Grimshaw, J. (1979). Complement selection and the lexicon. *Linguistic Inquiry*, *10*(2), 279–326.

Gross, C.G. (2002). Genealogy of the 'grandmother cell'. *The Neuroscientist*, *8*(5), 512–518.

Güngör, H. (2022). *That* solution to Prior's puzzle. *Philosophical Studies*, *179*, 2765–2785.

Hacker, P. (1982). Events and objects in space and time. *Mind*, *91*, 1–19.

Heim, I. (2000). Degree operators and scope. *Semantics and Linguistic Theory (SALT)*, *10*, 40–64.

Heim, I., & Kratzer, A. (1998). *Semantics in Generative Grammar*. Blackwell.

Hendriks, H. (1993). Studied Flexibility (Unpublished doctoral dissertation). University of Amsterdam.

Hendriks, H. (2020). Type shifting: The Partee triangle. In D. Gutzmann, L. Matthewson, C. Meier, H. Rullmann, & T. E. Zimmermann (Eds.), *The Companion to Semantics* (pp. 1–26). Wiley.

Higginbotham, J. (1983). The logic of perceptual reports. *The Journal of Philosophy*, *80*(2), 100–127.

Higginbotham, J. (2003). Remembering, imagining, and the first person. In A. Barber (Ed.), *Epistemology of Language* (pp. 496–533). Oxford University Press.

Hintikka, J. (1957). Modality as referential multiplicity. *Ajatus*, *20*, 49–64.

Hintikka, J. (1959). Existential presuppositions and existential commitments. *The Journal of Philosophy*, *56*(3), 125–137.

Hintikka, J. (1962). *Knowledge and Belief: An introduction to the logic of the two notions*. Cornell University Press.

Hintikka, J. (1969). Semantics for propositional attitudes. In *Models for Modalities*. (pp 87–111). Springer Dordrecht.

Hintikka, J. (1975). Impossible possible worlds vindicated. *Journal of Philosophical Logic*, *4*, 475–484.

Jacobson, P. (1999). Towards a variable-free semantics. *Linguistics and Philosophy*, *22*(2), 117–184.

Janssen, T.M.V. (1983). *Foundations and Applications of Montague Grammar* (Unpublished doctoral dissertation). Mathematical Center, University of Amsterdam.

Janssen, T.M., & Zimmermann, T.E. (2021). Montague semantics. In E.N. Zalta (Ed.), *The Stanford Encyclopedia of Philosophy*: Summer 2021 edition. Metaphysics Research Lab, Stanford University.

Jaszczolt, K.M. (2020). Human imprints of real time: From semantics to metaphysics. *Philosophia*, *48*(5), 1855–1879.

Kac, M.B. (1992). A simplified theory of Boolean semantic types. *Journal of Semantics*, *9*(1), 53–67.

Kaplan, D. (1976). How to Russell a Frege-Church. *The Journal of Philosophy*, *72*(19), 716–729.

Kastner, I. (2015). Factivity mirrors interpretation. *Lingua*, *164*, 156–188.

Keenan, E.L. (2015). Individuals explained away. In A. Bianchi (Ed.), *On Reference* (pp. 384–402). Oxford University Press.

Keenan, E.L. (2018). *Eliminating the Universe: Logical properties of natural language*. World Scientific.

Keenan, E.L., & Faltz, L.M. (1985). *Boolean Semantics for Natural Language* (Vol. 23). Springer.

Keil, F.C. (1979). *Semantic and Conceptual Development: An ontological perspective*. Harvard University Press.

King, J.C. (2002). Designating propositions. *Philosophical Review*, *111*(3), 341–371.

Klein, E. (1980). A semantics for positive and comparative adjectives. *Linguistics and Philosophy*, *4*(1), 1–45.

Klein, E., & Sag, I.A. (1985). Type-driven translation. *Linguistics and Philosophy*, *8*(2), 163–201.

Knuuttila, S. (2003). Medieval theories of modality. In E.N. Zalta (Ed.), *Stanford Encyclopedia of Philosophy: Fall 2003 edition*. Metaphysics Research Lab, Stanford University.

Köpping, J., & Zimmermann, T. E. (2020). Variables vs. parameters in the interpretation of natural language. In M. Sakamoto, N. Okazaki, K. Mineshima, & K. Satoh (Eds.), *New Frontiers in Artificial Intelligence* (pp. 164–181). Springer International Publishing.

Kracht, M. (2002). On the semantics of locatives. *Linguistics and Philosophy*, *25*(2), 157–232.

Kratzer, A. (1991). Modality. In A. von Stechow & D. Wunderlich (Eds.), *Semantics: An international handbook of contemporary research* (pp. 639–650). De Gruyter.

Kratzer, A. (1998). More structural analogies between pronouns and tenses. *Semantics and Linguistic Theory*, *8*, 92–110.

Kratzer, A. (2002). Facts: Particulars or information units? *Linguistics and Philosophy*, *5–6*(25), 655–670.

Kratzer, A. (2006). *Decomposing attitude verbs*. Manuscript. Jerusalem.

Kratzer, A. (2019). Situations in natural language semantics. In E. N. Zalta (Ed.), *Stanford Encyclopedia of Philosophy: Summer 2019 edition*. Metaphysics Research Lab, Stanford University.

Krifka, M. (1990). Four thousand ships passed through the lock: Object-induced measure functions on events. *Linguistics and Philosophy*, *13*(5), 487–520.

Kripke, S. (1981). *Naming and Necessity*. Blackwell Publishing.
Kripke, S. (1959). A completeness theorem in modal logic. *Journal of Symbolic Logic, 24*(1), 1–14.
Lahiri, U. (2002). *Questions and Answers in Embedded Contexts*. Oxford University Press.
Lambek, J. (1958). The mathematics of sentence structure. *American Mathematical Monthly, 65*(3), 154–170.
Landman, F. (1989a). Groups I. *Linguistics and Philosophy, 12*(5), 559–605.
Landman, F. (1989b). Groups II. *Linguistics and Philosophy, 12*(5), 723–744.
Landman, F. (2000). *Events and Plurality: The Jerusalem lectures*. Springer.
Landman, M. (2006). Variables in Natural Language (Unpublished doctoral dissertation). University of Massachusetts, Amherst.
Lassiter, D. (2012). Quantificational and modal interveners in degree constructions. *Semantics and Linguistic Theory (SALT), 22*, 565–583.
Lee, F. (1999). Evidence for tense in a 'tenseless' language. *Proceedings of the North East Linguistic Society, 29*, 229–246.
Lewis, D. (1972). General semantics. In D. Davidson & G. Harman (Eds.), *Semantics of Natural Language* (pp. 169–218). Springer.
Lewis, D. (1986). *On the Plurality of Worlds*. Blackwell.
Liefke, K. (2014). A Single-Type Semantics for Natural Language (Unpublished doctoral dissertation). Tilburg University.
Liefke, K. (2018). Relating intensional semantic theories: Established methods and surprising results. In S. Arai, K. Kojima, K. Mineshima, D. Bekki, K. Satoh, & Y. Ohta (Eds.), *New Frontiers in Artificial Intelligence*. JSAI-isAI 2017. Lecture Notes in Computer Science (Vol. 10838). Springer.
Liefke, K. (2019). A situated solution to Prior's substitution problem. Proceedings of *Sinn und Bedeutung, 23*, 55–72.
Liefke, K. (2021). Modelling selectional super-flexibility. *Semantics and Linguistic Theory (SALT), 31*, 324–344.
Liefke, K. (2024). Experiential attitudes are propositional. *Erkenntnis, 89*, 293–317.
Liefke, K., & Hartmann, S. (2018). Intertheoretic reduction, confirmation, and Montague's syntax-semantics relation. *Journal of Logic, Language and Information, 27*, 313–341.
Liefke, K., & Sanders, S. (2016). A computable solution to Partee's temperature puzzle. In M. Amblard, P. de Groote, S. Pogodalla, & C. Retoré (Eds.), *Logical Aspects of Computational Linguistics: Celebrating 20 years of LACL (1996–2016)* (pp. 175–190). Springer.
Liefke, K., & Werning, M. (2018). Evidence for single-type semantics: An alternative to e/t-based dual-type semantics. *Journal of Semantics, 35*(4), 639–685.

Link, G. (1983). The logical analysis of plural and mass terms: A lattice-theoretical approach. In R. Bäuerle, C. Schwarze, & A. von Stechow (Eds.), *Meaning, Use and Interpretation of Language* (pp. 302–323). De Gruyter.

Longley, J., & Normann, D. (2015). *Higher-Order Computability*. Springer.

Marten, L., & Kempson, R. (2002). Pronouns, agreement, and the dynamic construction of verb phrase interpretation: A dynamic syntax approach to Bantu clause structure. *Linguistic Analysis, 32*, 471–504.

Matthewson, L. (2006). Temporal semantics in a superficially tenseless language. *Linguistics and Philosophy, 29*(6), 673–713.

Matthewson, L. (2010). Cross-linguistic variation in modality systems: The role of mood. *Semantics and Pragmatics, 9*, 1–74.

McConnell-Ginet, S. (1973). Comparative Constructions in English: A syntactic and semantic analysis (Unpublished doctoral dissertation). University of Rochester.

McCormack, A. (2007). Subject and Object Pronominal Agreement in the Southern Bantu Languages: From a dynamic syntax perspective (Unpublished doctoral dissertation). University of London.

Mery, B., & Retoré, C. (2017). Classifiers, sorts, and base types in the Montagovian generative lexicon and related type theoretical frameworks for lexical compositional semantics. In S. Chatzikyriakidis & Z. Luo (Eds.), *Modern Perspectives in Type-Theoretical Semantics* (pp. 163–187). Springer.

Moltmann, F. (2003). Propositional attitudes without propositions. *Synthese, 135*(1), 77–118.

Moltmann, F. (2004). Two kinds of universals and two kinds of collections. *Linguistics and Philosophy, 27*, 739–776.

Moltmann, F. (2007). Events, tropes, and truthmaking. *Philosophical Studies, 134*, 363–403.

Moltmann, F. (2009). Degree structure as trope structure: A trope-based analysis of positive and comparative adjectives. *Linguistics and Philosophy, 32*, 51–94.

Moltmann, F. (2013a). *Abstract Objects and the Semantics of Natural Language*. Oxford University Press.

Moltmann, F. (2013b). Propositions, attitudinal objects, and the distinction between actions and products. *Canadian Journal of Philosophy, 43*(5–6), 679–701.

Moltmann, F. (2017). Attitude reports, cognitive products, and attitudinal objects: A response to G. Felappi 'On product-based accounts of attitudes'. *Thought: A Journal of Philosophy, 6*(1), 3–12.

Moltmann, F. (2020a). Existence predicates. *Synthese, 197*(1), 311–335.

Moltmann, F. (2020b). Truthmaker semantics for natural language. *Theoretical Linguistics*, *46*(3–4), 159–200.

Moltmann, F. (2022a). *Handouts from the class Natural Language Ontology (Université Côte d'Azur, Oct. 2022)*. www.friederike-moltmann.com/uploads/handout20120Philosophy20of20Language20NLO.docx.

Moltmann, F. (2022b). Natural language ontology. In E.N. Zalta (Ed.), *The Stanford Encyclopedia of Philosophy*: Winter 2022 edition. Metaphysics Research Lab, Stanford University.

Montague, M. (2007). Against propositionalism. *Noûs*, *41*(3), 503–518.

Montague, R. (1969). On the nature of certain philosophical entities. *The Monist*, *53*(2), 159–194.

Montague, R. (1970). Universal grammar. *Theoria*, *36*(3), 373–398.

Montague, R. (1973). The proper treatment of quantification in ordinary English. In J. Hintikka, P. Suppes, & J.M.E. Moravcsik (Ed.), *Approaches to Natural Language* (pp. 221–242). Dordrecht: Springer.

Morreau, M. (2014). Mr. Fit, Mr. Simplicity and Mr. Scope: From social choice to theory choice. *Erkenntnis*, *79*, 1253–1268.

Moulton, K. (2009). Natural Selection and the Syntax of Clausal Complementation (Unpublished doctoral dissertation). University of Massachusetts, Amherst.

Moulton, K. (2015). CPs: Copies and compositionality. *Linguistic Inquiry*, *46*(2), 305–342.

Mucha, A. (2013). Temporal interpretation in Hausa. *Linguistics and Philosophy*, *36*, 371–415.

Muskens, R. (1995). *Meaning and Partiality*. CSLI Publications.

Muskens, R. (2005). Sense and the computation of reference. *Linguistics and Philosophy*, *28*, 473–504.

Nebel, J.M. (2019). Hopes, fears, and other grammatical scarecrows. *The Philosophical Review*, *128*(1), 63–105.

Neeleman, A., van de Koot, H., & Doetjes, J. (2004). Degree expressions. *The Linguistic Review*, *21*, 1–66.

Palmer, G.B., & Woodman, C. (2000). Ontological classifiers as polycentric categories, as seen in Shona class 3 nouns. In M. Pütz & M. H. Verspoor (Eds.), *Explorations in Linguistics Relativity* (pp. 225–249). John Benjamins.

Parsons, T. (1972). Some problems concerning the logic of grammatical modifiers. In D. Davidson & G. Harman (Eds.), *Semantics of Natural Language* (pp. 127–141). Reidel.

Partee, B. (1973). Some structural analogies between tenses and pronouns in English. *The Journal of Philosophy*, *70*(18), 601–609.

Partee, B. (1983). Compositionality (technical report). Max-Planck-Institute of Psycholinguistics.

Partee, B. (1984). Nominal and temporal anaphora. *Linguistics and Philosophy, 7*(3), 243–286.

Partee, B. (1987). Noun phrase interpretation and type-shifting principles. In J. Groenendijk, D. de Jongh, J. Groenendijk, & M. Stokhof (Eds.), *Studies in Discourse Representation Theory and the Theory of Generalized Quantifiers* (pp. 115–143). Dordrecht.

Partee, B. (1992). Syntactic categories and semantic type. In M. Rosner & R. Johnson (Eds.), *Computational Linguistics and Formal Semantics* (pp. 97–126). Cambridge University Press.

Partee, B., & Rooth, M. (1983). Generalized conjunction and type ambiguity. In B. Partee & P. Portner (Eds.), *Formal Semantics: The essential readings* (pp. 334–356). Blackwell.

Pelletier, F.J. (2012). Lexical nouns are both +mass and +count, but they are neither +mass nor +count. In D. Massam (Ed.), *Count and Mass Across Languages* (pp. 9–26). Oxford University Press.

Piñón, C. (2008). From properties to manners: A historical line of thought about manner adverbs. *Linguistic Society of Belgium, 3,* 1–14.

Pollard, C. (2008). Hyperintensions. *Journal of Logic and Computation, 18*(2), 257–282.

Pollard, C. (2015). Agnostic hyperintensional semantics. *Synthese, 192,* 535–562.

Portner, P. (1992). Situation Theory and the Semantics of Propositional Expressions (Unpublished doctoral dissertation). University of Massachusetts, Amherst.

Potts, C. (2002). The lexical semantics of parenthical *as* and appositive *which*. *Syntax, 5*(1), 55–88.

Prior, A. (1963). Symposium: Oratio obliqua. *Proceedings of the Aristotelian Society, Supplementary Volumes, 37,* 115–146.

Prior, A. (1971). *Objects of Thought.* Clarendon Press.

Quine, W.V.O. (1948). On what there is. *The Review of Metaphysics, 2*(1), 21–38.

Quine, W.V.O. (1956). Quantifiers and propositional attitudes. *The Journal of Philosophy, 53,* 177–87.

Quine, W.V.O. (1960). *Word and Object.* New edition. The MIT Press.

Quiroga, R. Q., Reddy, L., Kreiman, G., Koch, C., & Fried, I. (2005). Invariant visual representation by single neurons in the human brain. *Nature, 435*(23), 1102–1107.

# References

Ramchand, G. (2022). Nonfinite verbal forms and natural language ontology. In D. Altshuler (Ed.), *Linguistics Meets Philosophy* (pp. 302–334). Cambridge University Press.

Rett, J. (2018). A typology of semantic entities. Handout from a talk at the PhLiP seminar.

Rett, J. (2022). A typology of semantic entities. In D. Altshuler (Ed.), *Linguistics Meets Philosophy* (pp. 277–301). Cambridge University Press.

Rips, L.J., & Hespos, S. J. (2019). Concepts of objects and substances in language. *Psychonomic Bulletin and Review, 26*, 1238–1256.

Ritchie, K. (2016). Can semantics guide ontology? *Australasian Journal of Philosophy, 94*(1), 24-41.

Roelofsen, F. (2008). Anaphora Resolved (Unpublished doctoral dissertation). University of Amsterdam.

Rothstein, S. (2020). Locations. *Journal of Semantics, 37*(4), 611–649.

Russell, B. (1905). On denoting. *Mind, 14*(56), 479–493.

Russell, B. (1996). *The Principles of Mathematics*. W. W. Norton & Company.

Schäfer, M. (2006). German Adverbial Adjectives: Syntactic position and semantic interpretation (Unpublished doctoral dissertation). University of Leipzig.

Schäfer, M. (2008). Resolving scope in manner modification. In O. Bonami & P. Cabredo Hofherr (Eds.), *Empirical Issues in Syntax and Semantics* (Vol. 7, pp. 351–372). CSSP.

Schönfinkel, M. (1924). Über die Bausteine der mathematischen Logik. *Mathematische Annalen, 92*, 305–316.

Selvik, K.-A. (2001). When a dance resembles a tree: A polysemy analysis of three Setswana noun classes. In H. Cuykens & B. Zawada (Eds.), *Polysemy in Cognitive Linguistics: Selected papers from the Fifth International Cognitive Linguistics Conference* (pp. 161–184). John Benjamins.

Sider, T. (2011). *Writing the Book of the World*. Oxford University Press.

Sinhababu, N. (2015). Advantages of propositionalism. *Pacific Philosophical Quarterly, 96*(2), 165–180.

Stalnaker, R. (1978). Assertion. In *Pragmatics* (pp. 315–332). Brill.

Stephenson, T. (2010). Vivid attitudes: Centered situations in the semantics of *remember* and *imagine*. *Semantics and Linguistic Theory (SALT), 20*, 147–160.

Stone, M. (1997). An Anaphoric Parallel between Modality and Tense (technical report). University of Pennsylvania, Department of Computer and Information Science.

Stowell, T. (1996). The phrase structure of tense. In J. Rooryck & L. Zaring (Eds.), *Phrase Structure and the Lexicon* (pp. 277–291). Springer.

Strawson, P. (1959). *Individuals: An essay in descriptive metaphysics*. Methuen.

Sutton, P.R. (2024). Types and type theories in natural language analysis. *Annual Review of Linguistics*, *10*, 107–126.

Thagard, P.R. (1978). The best explanation: criteria for theory choice. *The Journal of Philosophy*, *75*(2), 76–92.

Theiler, N., Roelofsen, F., & Aloni, M. (2018). A uniform semantics for declarative and interrogative complements. *Journal of Semantics*, *35*(3), 409–466.

Thomason, R.H. (1980). A model theory for the propositional attitudes. *Linguistics and Philosophy*, *4*(1), 47–70.

Tonhauser, J. (2011). Temporal reference in Paraguayan Guaraní. *Linguistics and Philosophy*, *34*, 257–303.

Uegaki, W., & Sudo, Y. (2019). The *hope-wh puzzle. *Natural Language Semantics*, *27*(4), 323–356.

Umbach, C., & Ebert, C. (2009). German demonstrative *so*: Intensifying and hedging effects. *Sprache und Datenverabeitung (International Journal for Language Data Processing)*, *1–2*, 153–168.

Umbach, C., & Gust, H. (2014). Similarity demonstratives. *Lingua*, *149*, 74–93.

Umbach, C., Hinterwimmer, S., & Gust, H. (2022). German *wie*-complements: Manners, methods and events in progress. *Natural Language and Linguistic Theory*, *40*, 307–343.

van Benthem, J. (1991). *Language in Action*. North-Holland.

van Lambalgen, M., & Hamm, F. (2005). *The Proper Treatment of Events*. Blackwell Publishing.

Vendler, Z. (1967a). Causal relations. *The Journal of Philosophy*, *64*(21), 704–713.

Vendler, Z. (1967b). *Linguistics in Philosophy*. Cornell University Press.

Vendler, Z. (1979). Vicarious experience. *Revue de Métaphysique et de Morale*, *84*(2), 161–173.

von Fintel, K., & Heim, I. (2021). *Intensional Semantics: Lecture notes for advanced semantics*. https://github.com/fintelkai/fintel-heim-intensional-notes/IntensionalSemantics.pdf.

von Stechow, A. (1984). Comparing semantic theories of comparison. *Journal of Semantics*, *3*(1), 1–77.

Wellwood, A. (2020). Interpreting degree semantics. *Frontiers in Psychology*, *10*(2972).

Williams, E.S. (1983). Against small clauses. *Linguistic Inquiry*, *14*(2), 287–308.

Winter, Y. (2002). *Flexibility Principles in Boolean Semantics: The interpretation of coordination, plurality, and scope in natural language.* MIT Press.

Winter, Y. (2005). Cross-categorical restrictions on measure phrase modification. *Linguistics and Philosophy, 28*, 233–276.

Wunderlich, D. (1991). How do prepositional phrases fit into compositional syntax and semantics? *Linguistics*, 591–622.

Wyner, A.Z. (1994). Boolean Event Lattices and Thematic Roles in the Syntax and Semantics of Adverbial Modification (Unpublished doctoral dissertation). Cornell University.

Zimmermann, T.E. (1993). On the proper treatment of opacity in certain verbs. *Natural Language Semantics, 1*(2), 149–179.

Zimmermann, T.E. (2001). Unspecificity and intensionality. In C. Féry & W. Sternefeld (Eds.), *Audiatur Vox Sapientiae: A Festschrift for Arnim von Stechow* (pp. 524–543). Akademie Verlag.

Zimmermann, T.E. (1987). Transparent adverbs and scopeless quantifiers. In J. Groenendijk, D. de Jongh, & M. Stokhof (Eds.), *Foundations of Pragmatics and Lexical Semantics* (pp. 81–99). Foris.

Zimmermann, T.E. (2006a). Monotonicity in opaque verbs. *Linguistics and Philosophy, 29*(6), 715–761.

Zimmermann, T.E. (2006b). The values of semantics. In P. Brandt & E. Fuß (Eds.), *Form, Structure, and Grammar* (Vol. 63, pp. 383–398). Akademie Verlag.

Zimmermann, T.E. (2018). Fregean compositionality. In D. Ball & R. Brian (Eds.), *The Science of Meaning: Essays on the metatheory of natural language semantics* (pp. 276–305). Oxford University Press.

Zimmermann, T.E. (2022). On Montague's 'The proper treatment of quantification in ordinary English'. In *A Reader's Guide to Classic Papers in Formal Semantics* (pp. 331–366). Springer.

Zimmermann, T.E., & Sternefeld, W. (2013). *Introduction to Semantics: An essential guide to the composition of meaning.* Mouton de Gruyter.

Zucchi, A. (2013). *The Language of Propositions and Events: Issues in the syntax and the semantics of nominalization* (Vol. 51). Springer.

Zwarts, J. (1997). Vectors as relative positions: A compositional semantics of modified PPs. *Journal of Semantics, 14*, 57–86.

Zwarts, J., & Winter, Y. (2000). Vector space semantics: A model-theoretic analysis of locative prepositions. *Journal of Logic, Language and Information, 9*, 169–211.

# Acknowledgements

This Element has greatly benefitted from discussions with Justin D'Ambrosio, Jan Köpping, Simon Kreutz, Dolf Rami, Emil Eva Rosina, Carla Umbach, Simon Vonlanthen, Markus Werning, Simon Wimmer, and Thomas Ede Zimmermann. I am grateful to David Kaplan and Barbara Partee for first raising my interest in natural language ontology. Four anonymous reviewers have improved this Element through their immensely helpful comments. I thank our student assistants Yonca Christine Klisch and Jonas Koopmann for their help with proofreading. Last, but certainly not least, I thank the series editors Jonathan Ginzburg and Daniel Lassiter for their trust, suggestions, and encouragement. Any remaining errors are my own.

*For Sam, to whom I promised that I would never write a book*

# Funding Statement

The author wishes to acknowledge funding from the German Federal Ministry of Education and Research BMBF (through her WISNA Professorship) and from the German Research Foundation DFG (through grant no. 397530566, as part of the research unit FOR 2812: *Constructing Scenarios of the Past*).

Cambridge Elements

# Semantics

### Jonathan Ginzburg
*Université Paris-Cité*

Jonathan Ginzburg is Professor of Linguistics at Université Paris-Cité (formerly Paris 7). He has held appointments at the Hebrew University of Jerusalem and King's College, London. He is one of the founders and currently associate editor of the journal *Dialogue and Discourse*. His research interests include semantics, dialogue, and language acquisition. He is the author of *Interrogative Investigations* (CSLI Publications, 2001, with Ivan A. Sag) and *The Interactive Stance: meaning for conversation* (Oxford University Press, 2012).

### Daniel Lassiter
*University of Edinburgh*

Daniel Lassiter is Senior Lecturer in Semantics in Linguistics & English Language at the University of Edinburgh. He works on topics at the intersection of formal semantics/pragmatics, cognitive psychology, and philosophy of language, including modality, conditionals, vagueness, scalar semantics, and Bayesian pragmatics. He is the author of *Graded Modality* (Oxford University Press, 2017) and numerous journal articles.

### About the Series

Elements in Semantics emphasizes the field's recent flourishing of interdisciplinary work, connecting linguistics and philosophy with cognitive science, computer science, neuroscience, law, anthropology, sociology, economics, and beyond. The series should be of interest to a broad community of researchers interested in the study of meaning from diverse perspectives.

# Cambridge Elements

# Semantics

## Elements in the Series

*Natural Language Ontology and Semantic Theory*
Kristina Liefke

A full series listing is available at: www.cambridge.org/ESEM

For EU product safety concerns, contact us at Calle de José Abascal, 56–1°,
28003 Madrid, Spain or eugpsr@cambridge.org.

www.ingramcontent.com/pod-product-compliance
Lightning Source LLC
LaVergne TN
LVHW022040260326
834688LV00061B/1659